TEACHING *with* digital video

WATCH · ANALYZE · CREATE

Edited by

GLEN L. BULL

LYNN BELL

International Society for Technology in Education
EUGENE, OREGON · WASHINGTON, DC

TEACHING *with* **digital video**

WATCH · ANALYZE · CREATE

Edited by **Glen L. Bull and Lynn Bell**

Director of Book Publishing: *Courtney Burkholder*
Acquisitions Editor: *Jeff V. Bolkan*
Production Editors: *Tina Wells, Lynda Gansel*
Production Coordinator: *Rachel Williams*
Graphic Designer: *Signe Landin*
Copy Editor: *Kristin Landon*
Proofreader: *Nancy Olson*
Indexer: *Pilar Wyman, Wyman Indexing*
Cover Design, Book Design, and Production: *Gwen Thomsen Rhoads*

Library of Congress Cataloging-in-Publication Data

Teaching with digital video : watch, analyze, create / Glen L. Bull, Lynn Bell, editors. – 1st ed.
    p. cm.
  ISBN 978-1-56484-266-4 (pbk.)
1. Digital video. 2. Interactive videos. 3. Educational technology. 4. Digital technology. I. Bull, Glen L. II. Bell, Lynn.
  LB1028.75.T43 2010
  371.33'46696—dc22

2010003694

First Edition
ISBN: 978-1-56484-266-4

Printed in the United States of America

International Society for Technology in Education (ISTE)
Washington, DC, Office:
  1710 Rhode Island Ave. NW, Suite 900, Washington, DC 20036-3132
Eugene, Oregon, Office:
  180 West 8th Ave., Suite 300, Eugene, OR 97401-2916
Order Desk: 1.800.336.5191
Order Fax: 1.541.302.3778
Customer Service: orders@iste.org
Book Publishing: books@iste.org
Book Sales and Marketing: booksmarketing@iste.org
Web: www.iste.org

Cover Images © iStockphoto.com (clockwise from top right): Grzegorz Choinski, Darren Hendley, Henrik Jonsson, Audrey Toutant, Rernd Wittelsbach
Northern Exposure stills © 1990 Universal Television Enterprises, Inc.

ISTE® is a registered trademark of the International Society for Technology in Education.

About ISTE

The International Society for Technology in Education (ISTE) is the trusted source for professional development, knowledge generation, advocacy, and leadership for innovation. ISTE is the premier membership association for educators and education leaders engaged in improving teaching and learning by advancing the effective use of technology in PK–12 and teacher education.

Home of the National Educational Technology Standards (NETS) and ISTE's annual conference and exposition (formerly known as NECC), ISTE represents more than 100,000 professionals worldwide. We support our members with information, networking opportunities, and guidance as they face the challenge of transforming education. To find out more about these and other ISTE initiatives, visit our website at **www.iste.org**.

As part of our mission, ISTE Book Publishing works with experienced educators to develop and produce practical resources for classroom teachers, teacher educators, and technology leaders. Every manuscript we select for publication is carefully peer-reviewed and professionally edited. We value your feedback on this book and other ISTE products. E-mail us at **books@iste.org**.

About the Editors

GLEN L. BULL is past president of the Virginia Society for Technology in Education and the Society for Information Technology and Teacher Education. He is a professor of instructional technology in the Curry School of Education at the University of Virginia and co-director of the Curry School Center for Technology and Teacher Education. He is co-editor of the online journal *Contemporary Issues in Technology and Teacher Education* and is co-editor of the book *Teaching with Digital Images* (ISTE, 2005).

LYNN BELL has worked with the Curry School of Education Center for Technology and Teacher Education at the University of Virginia for the past decade. She is co-editor of the online journal *Contemporary Issues in Technology and Teacher Education.* She has also co-edited the books *Teaching with Digital Images* and *Framing Research on Technology and Student Learning in the Content Areas.*

About the Contributors

CURBY ALEXANDER is an assistant professor of education at the University of Illinois at Springfield. His research interests include the use of technological innovations in history and social studies education, as well as the preparation of preservice and inservice teachers in all disciplines to use technology effectively in their instruction. Curby taught public school several years in Texas and Wyoming. His teaching and writing are grounded in his classroom experiences working with students of all ages, with technology, and with enrichment activities.

THOMAS C. HAMMOND is an assistant professor of education at Lehigh University in Bethlehem, Pennsylvania. He taught high school social studies for 10 years in the United States, Haiti, and Saudi Arabia. While he was a doctoral student at the University of Virginia, Tom was a designer, developer, and researcher of Primary Access (www.primaryaccess.org), the first online video editor designed for K-12 instruction. His current research and teaching focus on using technologies to enhance social studies instruction.

SARA B. KAJDER is an assistant professor of English education at Virginia Polytechnic Institute and State University (Virginia Tech). A former middle and high school English teacher, her current research includes the examination of the impact of adolescents' new literacies practices on their work as readers and writers inside and outside of the secondary English class-room. She is the author of *Bringing the Outside In: Visual Ways to Engage Reluctant Readers* and *Adolescents and Digital Literacies: Learning Alongside Our Students*.

JOHN K. LEE is an associate professor of social studies and middle grades education at North Carolina State University. He taught middle and high school for nine years and now, in addition to teaching social studies methods, conducts research on digital history. He is also interested in new literacies and creative uses of technology resources. He is author of the book *Visualizing Elementary Social Studies Methods* and co-author of the book *Guiding Learning with Technology*.

MARGARET "MAGGIE" L. NIESS is a professor emeritus of mathematics education in the Science and Mathematics Education Department at Oregon State University. Her research interests focus on the preparation of preservice and inservice teachers to teach with technology and the design of mathematics curriculum that integrates appropriate technologies as learning tools. She is co-author of the book *Guiding Learning with Technology*. She leads the design and implementation of an online MSP master's program for K–8 teachers.

JOHN C. PARK is an associate professor of science education at North Carolina State University. In 1979, John began using computer technology in his high school science classes by creating simulations using a TRS-80 computer. A few years later, he was building probeware using Apple computers for data collection and analysis in the physical sciences. His research interests now include investigating student learning while interacting with visual technologies such as microcomputer-based laboratories and interactive video. He investigates the effects of hands-on activities on learning and performance at all levels of the physical and Earth sciences.

BERNARD ROBIN is an associate professor in the Instructional Technology Program in the University of Houston's College of Education. He teaches courses on the integration of technology into the curriculum and educational uses of multimedia. He has published works on the emerging technologies in education and the professional development of teachers. He frequently works with K-12 students and teachers, as well as university educators to help them integrate technology into their teaching. Bernard is co-author of the book *The Educator's Guide to the Web* and is the creator of the Educational Uses of Digital Storytelling website (http://digitalstorytelling.coe.uh.edu).

DINA ROSEN is an assistant professor of early childhood education at Kean University, New Jersey. She has more than 10 years of teaching experience and has served as director of technology of a K-8 school. Her primary research interests include learning in technology-rich, digital age environments; social networking in early childhood years; and STEM education for young learners. Dina is also interested in qualitative research methods, especially the use of video and photo ethnography. She has published many peer-reviewed journal articles and book chapters. Her work has been presented at national and international conferences.

MICHAEL SEARSON is executive director of Kean University's School for Global Education and Innovation. Prior to his work in higher education, he was a classroom teacher. He continues to work closely with local school districts on projects involving innovative application of education technologies. In 2010, he was co-leader of a strand on Global Education at the National Technology Leadership Summit at the Punahou School in Hawaii. He was chairperson of the Xi Hu Conference on 21st Century Learning, held in Hangzhou, China, in November 2009. His work often connects local school districts with international partners.

DANIEL TILLMAN is a doctoral candidate in the instructional technology program at the University of Virginia and a graduate fellow with the Curry School Center for Technology and Teacher Education. Prior to coming to the University of Virginia, he directed and edited documentary films for eight years. Since 2005 he has served as an adjunct professor at George Mason University, where he teaches introduction to multimedia, advanced multimedia design, and documentary filmmaking. His current research focuses on the expansion of VisualEyes (www.viseyes.org) into the STEM content areas.

JANET M. WALKER is a professor of mathematics at Indiana University of Pennsylvania, where she has taught for the past 14 years. Prior to this she taught high school mathematics for eight years. She has presented extensively at state, regional, and national conferences on topics such as using technology in the mathematics classroom, gifted education, assessment, and implementation of the NCTM Standards in the classroom. She was an associate editor of the journal *School Science and Mathematics* for 10 years and co-editor of *PCTM (Pennsylvania Council of Teachers of Mathematics) Magazine* for 5 years.

CARL A. YOUNG, a former middle grades and secondary English teacher, is associate professor of English education at North Carolina State University. He teaches courses in English methods, teaching composition, content area reading and writing, and new literacies and emerging technologies. He conducts research on new literacies, participatory media, e-portfolios, and other technology applications in English education. Selected publications have appeared in *English Education*, *English Journal*, *Journal of Literacy Research*, and *Reading Psychology*. Carl is currently co-editing a book highlighting research in technology and English education.

Contents

INTRODUCTION

Glen L. Bull and Lynn Bell

teaching
with **digital video**

IN 2005, AT the time digital cameras were first becoming ubiquitous, we introduced the book *Teaching with Digital Images* to provide a framework for using digital images in the teaching and learning of the four core subject areas in the school curriculum.

Digital Video: A Ubiquitous Presence

THIS COMPANION book, *Teaching with Digital Video*, is appearing at a time of great technological and social change as well. The current generation of youth has been quick to innovate with digital video. According to YouTube (March 2010), more than 24 hours of video are uploaded to YouTube every minute (an increase from 10 hours per minute in March 2008), and youth are largely responsible for creating that content. According to the Digital Ethnography group at the University of Kansas (http://mediatedcultures.net), the typical contributor is a teenage author working outside school. The average length of each video is about three minutes, and 80% of the digital video clips are created by the users who post them.

Inexpensive, easy-to-use digital video cameras are accelerating this trend. With the Flip digital video camera, for example, users simply press the record button once to start recording and a second time to stop. A USB connector flips out and plugs directly into a computer to transfer the video. The camera functions as a flash drive and includes built-in video editing software. The software will also transfer video clips to YouTube or transmit them via e-mail.

The inclusion of video recording and viewing capabilities in mobile devices such as cell phones has had a profound effect on the spread of digital video as well. The ease of transfer across formats erases technological boundaries that formerly kept content confined to its originating medium. A video can be recorded on a cell phone video camera, edited with a cell phone application, and wirelessly uploaded to YouTube. As these technologies become more ubiquitous, intuitive, and affordable, digital videos are being created at an exponential rate.

As a result of technological advances, the definition of digital video is also broader than in the past. No longer is "video" limited to moving images filmed by a video camera. New technologies allow students to combine still images with their own narration for digital storytelling, construct digital animations such as Flash movies, and capture computer displays to create screencasts, resulting in new forms of digital video.

FULL ARTICLE

Klose's full article, "OK, Class, It's Time for YouTube," is available at www.csmonitor. com/2008/1117/ p19s03-hfes.html.

The availability of video on sites such as YouTube offers opportunities for learning and engagement that have never before existed. Much of what is called educational video on these sites merely features educators *talking*. Although the value in watching the world's most creative teachers discussing their favorite subjects is undeniable, the scope of the video's potential in education ranges much wider than the mere transmission of lectures.

Robert Klose (2008), a marine biology instructor in Maine, wrote about his experience with digital video in the *Christian Science Monitor*.

He begins:

NOTHING I SAY can do justice to these beautiful creations in their natural habitats. Yes, I can pass around some sharks' teeth, allow my students to handle a dried-out sponge, and let them take a gander at a small octopus preserved in a block of clear plastic. But there's a clear lack of dynamism here.

When his son introduced him to YouTube, Klose was a reluctant convert, resisting at first, commenting that he didn't want to watch "old rock bands." However, YouTube (and other video sites) has a nearly infinite variety of video on almost any conceivable topic, including "jellyfish with bioluminescent tentacles, octopi on the prowl, a scallop that swam like a set of animated dentures, sea cucumbers snuffling in the muck, flying fish soaring over the waves." Klose waited with great anticipation for an opportunity to use the clips in class. The result more than met his expectations.

THE EFFECT WAS MAGICAL. The blue ocean ebbed and flowed before us as myriad sea creatures swam, crawled, and flew about. I stood alongside the screen, narrating the action, occasionally pausing a video clip to point out this or that detail that illuminated my students' notes. ... The "wows" and "whoas" from the class confirmed for me that I had struck gold.

A Content-First Framework

DIGITAL VIDEO has now become a common feature of commercial, religious, political, and government contexts, as well as social interactions. In order for schools to remain relevant to students' lives and to the 21st-century workforce, educators must also seriously consider if and when digital video should be adapted for classroom use. An even more compelling argument for digital video may be made, however. Obviously, the mere existence of digital video will not, in and of itself, induce better learning. Yet an effective teaching method incorporating the right video may be one of the most successful means by which we can engage students' interest, help them understand a difficult concept, or improve their long-term retention of knowledge.

Student learning should be the primary objective for using digital video, and best practices with digital video may differ according to the curricular content to be learned. In the four subject-specific chapters of this book (Part 1, Chapters 1–4), you will find that each example activity begins by identifying the content or skill students will learn from the activity. Following the content description will be tips on how to use video technology most effectively and, then, an overview of the instructional strategy (or pedagogy).

Content: Digital Video across the Curriculum

DIGITAL VIDEO offers important new teaching and learning opportunities across the curriculum. Today, you can access and view millions of digital resources through the Internet: movie and TV clips, instructional videos, home movies of natural and cultural phenomena, and more. Analyses of digital video are made easier than ever by software that can overlay and combine representations to allow students to visualize underlying patterns. Using simple, free digital video tools, both you and your students can create video by combining photographs, documents, maps, audio clips, and even snippets of other videos. These capabilities allow students to explore concepts that would not be as accessible otherwise and add an important dimension to communication and conversations about these concepts.

Uses in mathematics, social studies, science, and language arts are discussed in Part 1. The best uses of digital video can vary dramatically from one content area to another. You might use video in language arts instruction very differently from the way you would use video in math instruction.

In math instruction, for example, digital video can be used to present challenging questions or improve students' visualization of mathematical concepts. It can offer opportunities for students to analyze situations and models leading to mathematical descriptions of relationships. Digital video, especially when it is layered with other interactive media, can also engage students in thinking about mathematics in ways that were previously difficult to achieve.

In social studies, on the other hand, digital video is taking its place alongside other forms of historical artifacts, such as photographs, maps, newspapers, and texts. Many social studies teachers already take advantage of documentaries and Hollywood films to investigate the big ideas of history, geography, economics, and civics. Video can add motion, sound, and a sense of real life to social studies instruction. You can even guide students through documentary projects in which they engage in critical thinking as they work with digitized primary sources, the raw materials of social studies.

In contrast to social studies, which focuses on history and human endeavors, science is primarily concerned with natural phenomena explored empirically, often through visual observation. In the science classroom, digital video—especially when enhanced by special effects such as time-lapse, slow-motion, and extreme closeup, or paired with data collected via probeware—provides a wide range of opportunities for engaging in scientific inquiry. Video allows students not only to see detail in a phenomenon that they might not otherwise be able to see, but it also invites repeated watching and application of science-process skills such as observing, inferring, classifying, predicting, measuring, communicating, and generating hypotheses.

In science, social studies, and mathematics, digital video is used as a mechanism for learning about a subject area. In language arts, digital media has become a facet of the subject area. This new mode of communication should be analyzed as well as utilized in learning. Students outside the classroom are increasingly consuming and creating multi-modal compositions that include images, sound, and digital video. Classroom projects using digital video offer an authentic framework for exploring the concepts of nonprint text and new literacies.

Because uses of digital video differ by subject area, this book approaches ideas for teaching with digital video by addressing each of the four core curriculum areas—mathematics, social studies, science, and English language arts—in separate chapters. Each chapter begins with an overview describing a variety of ways digital video can be used for teaching and learning specific to the subject area, followed by several activity descriptions that will catalyze your thinking about ways to use video in your instruction.

Although the book is structured to emphasize uses of video in specific subject areas, please don't limit yourself to reading only one content-area chapter. You'll be sure to find ideas in other chapters that you can adapt to multiple subjects and even to interdisciplinary projects.

Pedagogy: Student-Centered Classroom Uses of Digital Video

EACH OF the four subject-specific chapters in Part 1 of this book presents sample activities categorized according to the primary means by which students are engaged with the video: *watching*, *analyzing*, and *creating*. These verbs are not meant to specify steps in a process, nor are they exclusive. For example, students may both *watch* and *analyze* a video, or they may need to *create* a video before they can *analyze* it.

WATCHING

The traditional mode of teaching with digital video involved turning on a film projector (or laserdisc or VHS or DVD) and stepping out of the instructional role for the next 30 to 60 *minutes*. Today, the ease of presenting short, 30- to 60-*second* video clips allows you to pinpoint the most relevant information and play an active role in the instructional process. Locating video on the web to illustrate almost any phenomenon is relatively straightforward. Series of short video clips can easily be combined into a playlist specifically aligned to the needs of your students and the curriculum.

Watching digital video facilitates knowledge building, enabling students to acquire a better grasp of curricular concepts or adding to their understanding of the contexts surrounding instructional topics. For example, during science instruction students might view a precise moment in the eruption of a volcano or a close-up of a butterfly emerging from a chrysalis. In both science and mathematics instruction, video can set the context for an inquiry. In social studies instruction, students might view video of new cultures, geographic features, or reenactments of historical events. The videos may often be secondary sources, or interpretations of events, but could be primary sources as well.

In each case, you will need to guide students to be active watchers. *Watch* as used in this book is not a passive activity.

CRITICAL VIEWING

By Thomas C. Hammond and John K. Lee

A challenging point within this book is the difference between watching as a casual consumer and watching as a learner. Watching as a learner requires a form of critical viewing that incorporates at least two forms of awareness. The critical viewer must first be aware of the context of production—who made the video? When? Why? What genre does it fall into? In this sense, critical viewing is similar to media literacy, an awareness of the intentions embedded within media.

Whether watching a science instruction video or a political campaign commercial or a Hollywood film, students must be aware of the video's intent: This video is commanding your attention, and its creator had certain goals in mind, such as to deliver information, persuade, or entertain—or there may even have been multiple goals. Teachers should direct students' attention to these contexts before showing the video to the class.

The second layer of awareness in critical viewing is self-awareness. As viewers watch the presentation, how does information being viewed fit within each person's existing ways of knowing and understanding? What associations is the viewer making with previous knowledge? In what ways does the information confirm or conflict with this previous knowledge? How is the viewer being affected by the information in terms of its mood or tone? How does the viewer identify with the subject? What questions is the viewer left with?

Critical viewing of video parallels critical reading of texts. As with critical reading, critical viewing is mentally active and requires the viewer to be in dialogue with the material. The critical viewer is ready to challenge the video and engage it as a text or argument, not just as information or entertainment. Although these distinctions may not emerge naturally for students, as the teacher you can discuss critical viewing, encourage it, and even model it while viewing videos with your class.

ANALYZING

Activities that engage students in analysis of events can typically be classified as knowledge building as well. However, in these instances the students apply prior knowledge to reach a conclusion. In social studies the videos to be analyzed by students are often primary (i.e., original) sources. These might include user-generated content, political commercials and debates, or propaganda movies from prior eras. In mathematics, students can analyze video of physical objects moving or screencasts of Geometer's Sketchpad animations. (A screencast is a recording of the action taking place on a computer screen that can be replayed.) In science, a prerecorded event can be viewed multiple times and sped up or slowed down for analysis. Video can also be overlaid or paired with graphical or simulated data, supplying multiple representations. In language arts, video of student poetry slams, for example, can allow students to analyze the content of the presentations.

CREATING

Creating digital video typically is a form of knowledge expression—often divergent knowledge expression—which permits students more freedom and creativity as they synthesize and communicate what they have learned. Students have traditionally demonstrated their learning through composing lab reports in science and written essays in language arts. Creating digital video can also involve composing, through a written script, but with an added dimension. Students have become accustomed to communicating outside school using multiple forms of media that combine written language, audio, still images, and video (sometimes called *multimodal writing*). The same factors that make this form of communication engaging in other contexts can also be put to good use to address instructional objectives in school.

As attested to by the popularity of video sharing services such as YouTube, people enjoy creating video. Teaching strategies that engage students in creating digital video capitalize on students' desire to express themselves through this compelling medium and bring this energy into students' work with curricular content. Sites such as *Edutopia*'s Digital Generation Project (www.edutopia.org/digital-generation) and the International Student Media Festival (sponsored by the Association for Educational Communications and Technology; www.ismf.net) both illustrate the growing interest in student-created video and the range of student video production capability by age level.

Technology: New Tools, New Capabilities

INCORPORATING DIGITAL video in the classroom requires some technical skill. Therefore, we have included three chapters in Part 2 of the book providing an overview of the tools and techniques needed to acquire and create digital video, as well as ways to take advantage of new opportunities to communicate with and about video.

ACQUIRING DIGITAL VIDEO

You and your students may acquire digital video for classroom use in a variety of ways:

- Obtain original footage with a digital or still camera, cell phone, webcam, or screen capture software

- Go to websites where digital videos are stored (you can either watch from the website or download video to your computer)

- Combine a collection of still images, enhanced with pans and zooms and even narration and background music

- Digitize television broadcasts or VHS movies

- Extract video from a DVD

BLOCKED SITES

Note that many school networks block YouTube and similar sites, and with good reason. A great deal of content on the web is not appropriate for students or school use. You may need to search for appropriate video clips from home or at some other site away from school.

Once you have identified relevant content, there is the matter of getting it into your classroom. Fortunately, a number of different software applications can be used to download streaming video clips from the web. Once you have downloaded the file, you can transfer it to your laptop, a CD, or a portable hard drive. One benefit of capturing the content in this way is that you will be able to present relevant video clips to your class even when Internet access is unavailable or unreliable. A more detailed description of this process is provided in Chapter 6: "Acquiring Digital Video."

CREATING DIGITAL VIDEO

The title of Chapter 7–"Creating Digital Video"–refers to taking video that you have acquired and transforming it into a form that is educationally useful. For example, if you film your own footage, you will likely need to edit it to a more watchable length. If you are using video obtained from other sources, you may need to trim it, rearrange scenes, or combine it with other video clips. We provide an overview of tools and general techniques for accomplishing the following tasks:

- Making a movie from still images alone

- Extracting clips of specific scenes from longer video

- Trimming or deleting unwanted video footage

- Rearranging scenes in a video

- Combining multiple video clips or combining video and still images

- Adding special effects and transitions to your video

- Adding sounds, music, or voice-over narration to your video

- Adding text-only frames or adding text captions to images or video

In addition, screencasting software such as Camtasia and Captivate allows you to create interactive quizzes associated with video content, permitting students to assess their understanding of content viewed. Screencasts also offer capabilities that cannot be easily replicated in a live presentation. Screencasting software makes it convenient to add callouts (arrows and bubbles to highlight features of interest), captions, and annotations to the video. It also lets you zoom in to a specific section of the screen or pan across from one section of the screen to another. Other features, such as "picture-in-picture" (for example, a headshot of a narrator inset into the larger screen), are also supported.

The resulting product can be customized for dissemination on a traditional DVD or CD, transmitted to the web or a video service such as YouTube (or educational equivalents such as TeacherTube), transferred to a video iPod, or simply saved to a portable hard drive.

COMMUNICATING: CONTEXT FOR A SOCIAL MEDIUM

The Pew Internet and American Life Project reports that digital video has also become a social medium. Youth are not only posting video, but also employing it as a springboard for dialogue and conversations through associated comments and embedded posts and reposts in blogs and other websites.

Researchers working within the Pew Foundation note that the desire to share a viewing experience with others plays an important role in the spread of online video. The majority of online video viewers share links to online video with others. The Internet and American Life Project reports that "young adults are the most 'contagious carriers' in the viral spread of online video" (Madden, 2007, p. 6).

The ultimate goal of digital video is communication. A new generation increasingly uses video in the way that previous generations may have used postcards—as a fast and easy way to connect. We increasingly use digital video in this manner in our teaching and professional interactions at the university. A short video clip combined with a background document can quickly provide information, an instructional process, or an illustration of student engagement in a manner that would be difficult to capture in any other way.

Much of this communication takes place on the Internet—via Facebook, blogs, Twitter links, and other social media. This activity contrasts with schools, where the cell phones may be blocked and the Internet may be down or intermittent for several days at a time. Teachers who use video should be aware of ways in which digital video can be linked or embedded in a class web page, blog, or wiki. Some of these uses are discussed in Chapter 8: "Communicating with Digital Video."

Because of this shifting social context, organizations as varied as the National Science Foundation and the MacArthur Foundation are extremely interested in boundaries between formal and informal learning. Chapter 5 ("Digital Video and Informal Learning: Turning the Lens Outside the Classroom") discusses opportunities in the area of using digital video in informal learning settings.

The SITE Screening Room

READERS OF this book might expect to find an accompanying CD, as is the case with *Teaching with Digital Images*. Instead, all the videos and resources developed by the authors of *Teaching with Digital Video* are provided online through the SITE Screening Room (http://site.aace.org/video/books/teaching), a service provided by the Society for Information Technology and Teacher Education (SITE). We will provide updates and new resources through the SITE Screening Room as they become available after publication of this book. New video editing software, tools, and techniques are becoming available at a rapid pace. For this reason, specific techniques that apply to a specific software edition or version are provided through the SITE Screening Room, where they can be updated as new versions appear. This online resource will also allow educators to submit, view, and discuss educational digital videos in a variety of content areas. If you are involved in engaging work with digital video in your teaching, we hope that you will share your expertise on this site.

In order to recognize and support your work, each year SITE will recognize outstanding instructional uses of digital video in K-12 subject areas—science, mathematics, language arts, and social studies. If you or your students have created a noteworthy or innovative video in a content area, we encourage you to submit the video to the SITE Screening Room. Awards recognizing exemplary uses will be announced at the SITE annual conference each spring and posted on the SITE website (http://site.aace.org).

Conclusion

TONY WAGNER (2008), in his book the *Global Achievement Gap*, said that today's students and young workers want to be "interactive producers, not isolated consumers…. They long to interact," and they "long to learn and to create in a collaborative, collegial environment" (p. 188). These young people are engaged by learning through multimedia and connections to others, approaching learning as discovery, and learning by creating, according to Wagner. In the following chapters, you will find a number of ideas for using digital video to facilitate these very kinds of learning experiences. The ultimate objective is to harness and focus the energies of your students, so, as Wagner suggested, they will use their skills with digital technologies to, "make significant contributions to our society as learners, workers, and citizens" (p. 187).

References

Klose, R. (2008, November 17). OK, class, it's time for YouTube. *Christian Science Monitor.* Retrieved from www.csmonitor.com/2008/1117/p19s03-hfes.html

Madden, M. (2007). *Online video.* Washington, DC: Pew Internet & American Life Project.

Wagner, T. (2008). *The global achievement gap: Why even our best schools don't teach the new survival skills our children need—And what we can do about it.* New York, NY: Basic Books.

YouTube (2010, March 17). Oops pow surprise…24 hours of video all up in your eyes! [Blog post]. Retrieved from http://youtube-global.blogspot.com/2010/03/oops-pow-surprise24-hours-of-video-all.html

PART 1

using
digital video
across the
curriculum

CHAPTER 1

Thomas C. Hammond and
John K. Lee

digital video in social studies education

THE BACKBONE of social studies instruction is media. The big ideas of history, geography, economics, and civics have been powerfully expressed in documentary, Hollywood film, and pictorial form. As a social studies teacher, you may already use classic resources such as Matthew Brady's Civil War photographs or maps from Ortelius' 16th-century atlas to make videos. You might also use excerpts from movies such as Charlie Chaplin's *Modern Times* or documentaries such as Ken Burns' *Civil War*. These sources are not only significant historical artifacts (the first battlefield photographs, the first world atlas, and a massively popular social protest film) but also powerful teaching tools. Skillful teachers use these resources and others—often in a digital format—to bring social studies alive for students through their compelling visuals.

Today, digital video is taking its place alongside other forms of

FIGURE 1.1. Examples of historical artifacts that are also visual media for instruction.

media as a record of significant historical events. On the subject of the Iraq War, entire documentaries have been created using only amateur video shot by soldiers. In 2007, CNN's "YouTube Debates" brought homemade digital video into the heart of national political campaigns. Digital video, even in lower-quality forms, can trigger social and political action, as demonstrated by the events following the 1991 arrest and beating of Rodney King in Los Angeles and in the 2006 collapse of Virginia Senator George Allen's re-election campaign. Examples of historically significant digital videos will continue to multiply as digital video cameras in one form or another—handheld, cell phone, webcam, and so forth—make their way into every household and public space (and classroom!) in the world.

Digital video also poses important new teaching opportunities for social studies teachers. Using a simple, free digital video editor, you can compose a documentary on your computer, mixing together photographs, documents, maps, audio clips, and even snippets of other videos. Alternatively, you can facilitate student project work. For example, students can compose a short film about the Civil War drawing upon Brady's photographs (Figure 1.2), scanned soldiers' letters and battlefield maps, period music, and contemporary video recorded at battle sites or re-enactments. The medium of digital video opens up possibilities for both you and your students.

As mentioned in the introduction, digital video can include a wide range of media, such as film, video captured with a camera, and still images with motion added. We will look at these and other types of digital video in various content-based instructional settings, but first we will review some of the strengths and weaknesses of the digital video medium for social studies instruction.

Content-Based Instructional Settings for Digital Video Use

RATHER THAN simply relying on the text-intensive treatments available in your textbook and supplemental materials, you can use video to add motion, sound, and a sense of real life to your instruction. For example, in a unit about Latin America, traditional resources would include print texts supplemented with maps and perhaps flags of the region. Consider, however, the possibilities for enhancing the unit with feature films that bring the cultures to life as students watch (Vanden, 2007). Students might even watch

FIGURE 1.2. Working from primary sources to create a digital movie.

video produced by the very people participating in the events or located in the places being studied. If you are teaching a unit on Haiti, for example, you can find YouTube videos made by people in Haiti that show transportation systems, markets, Carnival celebrations, beaches, and even news reports from the country. Participant video content can provide unique teaching opportunities, such as when you show footage taken by cruise ship patrons landing on fenced-off beaches in the north and contrasting it with scenes from food riots in the capital.

As described in the introduction, you can create your own video content for students to watch, too. For example, in a geography lesson, you can create a video that draws upon local features to illustrate concepts such as landforms, location, or movement. By integrating local references into the lesson, you are both building students' interest in the content and helping students anchor their understanding of the concepts in familiar reference points.

Digital video is also useful for compressing content, which can be vital in coverage-oriented fields such as history. Research has demonstrated that students learn more from a combination of words and pictures than from text alone (Mayer, 2005), and by selecting only the key sections of a video, you can use the minimal instructional time to achieve the maximum content exposure. For example, rather than show an entire documentary on World War I, you can create a customized version addressing the exact concepts specified within the curriculum. Some video services such as Discovery Education (http://streaming.discoveryeducation.com) make this process easier by cutting full-length videos into individual chapters or clips.

You can engage students in critical thinking and analysis using digital video as well. Although an emerging body of research suggests that students are deeply, often unconsciously, influenced by what they see in films (for example, see Dimitriadis, 2000), you can design activities to counteract this passive absorption of information and emotions. For example, base a study of American presidential elections on a set of campaign commercials, such as those available from the Museum of the Moving Image (www.livingroomcandidate.org). By guiding the class through a careful analysis of selected commercials, you can help students progress as scholars, citizens, and media consumers. This approach can also be used with commercial films, where students learn to "read" films as primary sources rather than viewing them as an authority or a re-creation of reality.

The most powerful way to immerse students in critical thinking using digital video is to engage them in authorship, or creating their own video. As students compose a documentary using historical artifacts, they learn the content, develop their research and primary source analysis skills, and even come to understand the interpretive nature of historical accounts. An ambitious teacher can even have students "re-cut" a finished documentary to provide alternate emphasis—sometimes just by rearranging the visuals or using a different motion over an image.

Limitations of Digital Video

USING DIGITAL video in social studies instruction has limitations as well. In terms of its mechanics, video is a linear format: it progresses frame by frame, second by second, from the beginning to the end of the clip. In terms of content, instructional videos are often unidimensional, conveying only one idea at a time. Although these characteristics of linearity and focus can be useful in directing students' attention, they can also be a trap. When learning history, for example, students often struggle to understand how different issues and events unfold simultaneously, how living conditions can vary widely within the same region, and how events emerge from multiple and conflicting influences and not linear chains of causation.

If a film focuses on a single sequence of events or suggests a linear chain of causation, it may reinforce students' misconceptions rather than challenge them. Students may arrive in your classroom with preconceptions about watching videos stemming from their experiences watching movies, television, and Internet-based media. Rather than viewing a video with the intended critical eye and careful ear for content, your students may apply habits formed during recreational media consumption. If, for example, students view footage from a Vietnam battlefield and think of it as a Hollywood action sequence, they will miss the point that this is a real war—they are watching tragedy, not entertainment.

A reflective teacher will, therefore, consider how to compensate for these disadvantages when using digital video. Before showing a video to students, differentiate between watching a video as a casual viewer and watching as a scholar. You may also wish to explain to students the learning purpose of the video and their expected behaviors (for example, watching and analyzing, or creating).

You can interrupt the video. In a geography lesson about regions, for example, you could stop and restart the video or select key frames that focus on other geographic themes, such as movement or place. For a history lesson about triangular trade, you might use clips from multiple sources to discuss or illustrate the different aspects of the trade routes rather than rely on a single video.

SOCIALLY NETWORKED VIDEO AND
A NEW LANDSCAPE FOR U.S. CITIZENSHIP

By Michael Searson

Recent events suggest that engagement with emergent media and digital video might become important elements of active and responsible citizenship.

During and since the historic 2008 campaign for the U.S. presidency, the impact of socially networked digital video (e.g., YouTube) has seemed ubiquitous. In fact, near the end of the presidential campaign, the popular political website Politico posted a selection of campaign-related videos it called "the 10 most viral videos of the campaign" (www.politico.com/news/stories/1108/15182.html).

As defined by Wikipedia, a viral video "is a video clip that gains widespread popularity through the process of Internet sharing, typically through e-mail or instant messaging, blogs and other media-sharing websites." In other words, these videos gain their notoriety because they are shared widely among users of the Internet. Certainly, the 2008 presidential campaign was replete with examples of socially networked videos that grabbed headlines for days (and sometimes weeks), such as the video showing the fiery sermons of the Reverend Jeremiah Wright.

Shortly after he was elected, President Barack Obama posted his first weekly address to the website he set up during the transition period from the election to his inauguration (www.change.gov, which is no longer accessible). This site contained a number of socially networked tools that allowed users to view and make comments and suggestions as the transition team prepared to assume governance. Even after moving into the White House, President Obama has continued this practice of posting digital videos of his addresses to social networks.

Although the Whitehouse.gov site is somewhat less Web 2.0 oriented than the change.gov site, a White House YouTube channel was created (www.youtube.com/user/whitehouse) that makes full use of Web 2.0 tools. For example, the president's weekly address videos are posted to this site, which also allows viewers to submit comments. Additionally, as the White House unveiled its economic stimulus plan, it launched a website, www.recovery.gov, where citizens can track how stimulus monies are being spent and even make suggestions to help the economy.

It appears that citizenship in the United States (and likely in other parts of the world) will increasingly become connected to digital video-related literacy in Web 2.0 environments. Imagine a classroom project that draws the attention of the White House. For example, in the "Share your recovery story" section on the Recovery.gov website, students and teachers could document community stories and submit them. The larger story to be told is that the U.S. president and the White House have fully embraced digital video and social networking tools. Educators should do the same!

Digital Video Activities in Social Studies

THE SELECTED pedagogical themes of this book—watch, analyze, and create—are designed to provide a lens for making the most of your instructional use of digital video. What follows are three detailed instructional examples of how digital video can be used in social studies. In presenting these examples we seek to highlight digital video in the context of rich content and authentic classroom settings. Each activity will highlight the actions of the students. As you read, observe the ways in which you can use digital video to enhance or compress content and engage students in critical thinking, thus avoiding shallow or passive modes of student interaction.

Watching Digital Video Activity

THE POSSIBILITIES for using digital video in social studies are truly endless. As historian Gary Nash noted, today teachers and students have "at their fingertips ... millions of photographs, paintings, sculptures, buildings, primary documents, film clips, and secondary readings that spring into one's computer screen through thousands of Internet websites" (Percoco, 1998, p. xiii). These digital sources can provide opportunities to engage students in powerful and authentic social studies instruction.

FIGURE 1.3. Charlie Chaplin (as The Tramp) in a scene from the 1921 movie *The Kid*.

Charlie Chaplin's character The Tramp (or Little Tramp) is one of the most recognizable symbols of the silent film era. Over the course of two decades of film appearances, the character became an American cultural icon, evoking individualism and longing amidst the turmoil of 20th-century life. The Tramp made his final appearance in *Modern Times* in 1936. This film frequently appears on lists of the greatest American movies, and several sequences from the film have become part of the foundation of comedic film. The film makes a great tool for teaching about the social and political aspects of the Great Depression.

Modern Times
American History
GRADE LEVEL: 11

Objectives

- Students will be able to describe the economic uncertainties facing Americans in the 1930s, both in terms of employment and in the role of technology.

- Students will understand that film is a historical source that reflects the cultural context of its production as well as the viewpoint of its creators/financiers.

National Council for the Social Studies Thematic Strands Addressed

VI Power, authority, and governance

VII Production, distribution, and consumption

VIII Science, technology, and society

X Civic ideals and practices

National Educational Technology Standards for Students (NETS·S) Addressed

1. **Creativity and Innovation**

    a. apply existing knowledge to generate new ideas, products, or processes

4. **Critical Thinking, Problem Solving, and Decision Making**

    a. plan strategies to guide inquiry

6. **Technology Operations and Concepts**

    a. understand and use technology systems

Technology/Materials Needed

- DVD or online video of *Modern Times*

CONTENT

Modern Times can be used to address many content areas, from civics to economics to history. Here, the film is used to address American history, specifically the Great Depression (1929-39). In the film, Chaplin, who was simultaneously the writer, director, producer, and star, expresses the fears and hopes that society experienced during those uncertain times. The film captures ideas common during the Great Depression, such as the tenuous nature of employment, struggles over unions (e.g., the International Workers of the World), and attacks on socialist or communist organizations (e.g., Palmer Raids of 1919). By watching *Modern Times*, students can consider the human side of the Depression.

TECHNOLOGY

Modern Times is available in a variety of formats, including DVD and online clips. Using these formats will allow you to control stopping and starting points more easily and to rapidly leap from one scene to another. If you are showing the film on a DVD, you can do this manually, provided that you are able to skillfully fast-forward and pause as needed. If you are showing the film via a media player (e.g., Windows Media Player), you can move the cursor to the correct starting times. Finally, the film is available (in sections) on YouTube; you can arrange the clips in order and skip ahead using the cursor. Note that the resolution of the online clips may not be high enough for students to pick up details of facial expressions and body language. We recommend finding a copy of the DVD at your local library.

PEDAGOGY

Although students will enjoy watching Chaplin and may already be familiar with the character and some of the scenes, their work will require careful scaffolding so that they will grasp how the action on-screen connects to the larger framework of American life and ideas during the 1930s. The activity described here is designed to engage students in a critical, reflective form of watching. You will be asking them to do something challenging and very different from what they normally do. Students will watch the film and (we hope!) enjoy the comedy, but they will also note where the action on screen parallels events in real life and what ideas or people from history are portrayed in the film. There may also be moments when the students are confused or have questions.

Before beginning the movie, you should check for students' prior knowledge about the Depression era, and especially the character of The Tramp. Also, before beginning the study of the film, you should describe for students its use of sound. *Modern Times* has been identified as one of the last silent movies, but it is only quasi-silent. Sound effects and music are used, and there is some spoken dialogue and even singing. However, in these instances, the voice is not fully synchronized to the film, and pantomime and music are still the primary storytelling vehicles. These concepts should be explained in advance to the students; otherwise, questions might arise in the middle of a sequence when students are supposed to be focusing on content.

Finally, you should situate the movie within its time period: the 1930s, during the Great Depression. Again, ask students to discuss what they know about this era and identify the topics and events that they expect to see in the film.

Once you are ready to begin, distribute to the students a sheet with the text from the title cards in the scenes you are showing. As a silent (or quasi-silent) film, title cards were used to set up each scene. This text will serve both to introduce the characters (e.g., "The gamin—a child of the waterfront, who refuses to go hungry") and to structure students' discussion of the movie. As you reach these title cards, you can pause the film to explore the ideas presented.

We suggest showing only sections of the film. For this activity, four scenes are most relevant:

- The opening, which is focused on The Tramp's factory work

- A scene that involves Chaplin's interactions with the police and prison system

- A scene with his wife that focuses on their visions of a happy future

- The closing scene

The film's opening (about 15 minutes) helps establish the key elements of the film, including the setting, characters, tone, and theme.

- The *setting* is an urban, industrialized, technological society, and, specifically, the factory of the Electro Steel Corp.

- The *main characters* are The Tramp and The Gamin, played by Paulette Goddard, Chaplin's real-life wife at the time.

- The *tone* is expressed through both the music (ominous horns and dramatic strings–not a score that suggests slapstick comedy) and the opening shots (a ticking clock, a flock of sheep moving forward intercut with crowds of workers exiting a subway and entering a factory).

- The *theme* is delivered explicitly through a title card: "A story of industry, of individual enterprise–humanity crusading in the pursuit of happiness."

Beyond establishing the key elements, the opening scene of *Modern Times* can be used to initiate discussion about industrialization and working conditions in the 1930s. In the opening scene, The Tramp suffers a nervous breakdown while working, ultimately running amok throughout the factory (approximately 15 minutes into the film). Ask students to recap the big ideas presented in the opening scene. These may include industrialization, efficiency, and dehumanization.

Encourage students to draw a contrast between the pain and anguish demonstrated by Chaplin's character and the factory owner's vision of happiness, which is an automated eating machine that will help his workers to keep working nonstop, thus allowing him to "get ahead of [his] competition." This is the heart of Chaplin's critique of 20th-century life: when taken to its extreme, industrialization dehumanizes people and literally drives them insane. This anti-mechanization perspective was a common theme in the 1930s (see, for example, William Ogburn's *You and Machines* [1934]). Especially insightful students may be able to make the connection between Chaplin's dim view of technological progress expressed in the film (e.g., the sales pitch comes from a "mechanical salesman," and the inventor pantomimes speaking) and Chaplin's refusal to embrace spoken dialogue.

After showing the first 15 minutes of the film, you can skip ahead to The Tramp's release from the hospital. The title card for this scene says, "Cured of a nervous breakdown but without a job, he leaves the hospital to start life anew." The subsequent action shows Chaplin being confused for a communist and thrown in jail. At this point we recommend skipping further ahead to the title card "Happy in his comfortable cell" (approximately 10 minutes), showing The Tramp lolling on his prison bunk, reading about strikes and riots outside the jail. The Tramp is freed from prison but begs to stay. ("Can't I stay a little longer? I'm so happy here.") At this point, you may have to stop the film to explain the reason he is being pardoned (he helped quell a prison riot), and you should also discuss the viewpoint being suggested by Chaplin that life outside the prison is worse than life inside. Inside the prison, you are fed and sheltered; outside the prison, you are on your own.

Following his release from prison, skip ahead to the point where The Tramp and his wife, The Gamin (a take on *gamine*, which is French word for a homeless girl), have met and are envisioning a future together (approximately 40 minutes into the film). Sitting in a suburb, The Tramp asks, "Can you imagine us in a little home like that?" The following dream sequence presents a vision of Utopia in which the two characters are living happily together in a neat, suburban house. A cow provides milk, and grapes are growing immediately outside the door. Dinner is a massive steak, and the scene transitions back to reality with Chaplin pretending to eat it. This scene captures the middle class aspirations of the 1920s, such as the Republicans' 1928 presidential campaign ads featuring "a chicken in every pot." You may wish to revisit this scene when discussing suburban life in the 1950s and '60s, when this accomplishment was first realized on a large scale—employment for unskilled and semiskilled labor was steady and wages were high enough for workers to become homeowners. In the depths of the Great Depression, however, it appeared to be a dream.

Close the viewing by showing the last scene of the film: The Tramp and The Gamin sit by a road, disconsolate. When The Gamin asks, "What's the use of Trying?" she is cheered by The Tramp, who says, "Buck up—never say die. We'll get along!" The two walk off, arm-in-arm into the sunset. You can situate this scene in the political promise expressed by Franklin Roosevelt at the time that, although no one knew how the Depression would end, the people would persevere. You can discuss Roosevelt's Fireside Chats as a national form of encouragement (e.g., 1934's "On Moving Forward to Greater Freedom and Greater Security").

Note that this activity does *not* require showing the entire film but rather selected scenes. The primary ideas in the activity can be conveyed using only a few key scenes. In a film class, you would want to show the entire movie. For a social studies class, on the other hand, you should show only what you need. Think of yourself as an editor. Just as Chaplin cut out scenes to focus the film on selected ideas and characters, you will do the same, making selections for the purposes of social studies content learning.

MORE IDEAS FOR WATCHING DIGITAL VIDEO IN SOCIAL STUDIES

■ View documentaries that include multiple perspectives. For example, *They Marched into Sunlight* is an award-winning book and documentary, available from PBS, that provides a rich treatment of the Vietnam War. The title explores two events in October 1967: (1) an ambush of an American battalion 40 miles outside of Saigon and (2) an antiwar demonstration at the University of Wisconsin-Madison that turned into a riot. This dual focus allows students to see multiple aspects of the conflict—the war in Vietnam versus the war at home, supporters versus opponents, people's actions and statements at the time versus their beliefs after decades of reflection.

■ View feature films that present unfamiliar perspectives on issues. As an example, consider the topic of illegal immigration. *El Norte* (1983) is a narrative of two siblings who flee Guatemala for the United States. The Belgian film *La Promesse* (1997) is set in Western Europe and focuses on the demiworld of those who provide services to the illegal immigrants. As with any film, be sure to screen these titles in advance to see whether the nature of the language and imagery is acceptable within your school, and consider omitting scenes for the purposes of appropriateness or time constraints.

Analyzing Digital Video Activity

TRANSPORTATION SYSTEMS are both ubiquitous and invisible. We see and use multiple transportation systems every day, but we also tend not to think about them. They are familiar, so they recede into the background. In contrast, consider the excitement of a child just learning about transportation and related words as he or she calls out, "Truck! Train! Airplane!" Additionally, we tend to understand only the transportation networks we are directly familiar with. A child who has grown up in the suburbs may understand cars and the road system but may have little conception of high-density urban subways and buses as a dominant mode of commuter transportation. Commercial transportation, such as long-haul freight and local agriculture, may also be entirely unfamiliar to children or understood in only a superficial sense.

Digital video provides a powerful opportunity to visualize different transportation networks around the world, giving students a window into culture, economics, and government. This activity uses as its starting point two videos about trains in Tokyo, Japan. As with all the activities described in this chapter, many permutations are possible, such as different starting points or final projects focused on other transportation networks.

Transportation Systems
Social Studies—Transportation Systems
GRADE LEVELS: 5–8

Objectives

- Students will be able to identify contrasting cultural patterns in transportation systems and cultural expectations or patterns of behavior.

- Students will be able to identify and explain patterns of historical change over time and connect them to changes in policy and/or economics.

National Council for the Social Studies Thematic Strands Addressed

III People, places, and environments

VII Production, distribution, and consumption

VIII Science, technology, and society

National Educational Technology Standards for Students (NETS·S) Addressed

1. **Creativity and Innovation**

   a. apply existing knowledge to generate new ideas, products, or processes

2. **Communication and Collaboration**

   c. develop cultural understanding and global awareness by engaging with learners of other cultures

4. **Critical Thinking, Problem Solving, and Decision Making**

   a. identify and define authentic problems and significant questions for investigation

   c. collect and analyze data to identify solutions and make informed decisions

6. **Technology Operations and Concepts**

   a. understand and use technology systems

Technology/Materials Needed

Digital videos available online on YouTube:

- Actually Full Train in 1991 (Why Flex Time is a Good Idea)—
  www.youtube.com/watch?v=Lf8Ig2M3Zq0

- Less Crowded in 2008—www.youtube.com/watch?v=8ScexNfYbBQ

CONTENT

Students in the United States may not be familiar with the phenomenon of "train packing." This practice originated in Japan on the commuter rail systems running through densely populated urban areas. The rides on tightly packed trains are uncomfortable and unpleasant, but they serve to move millions of people around cities each day. White-gloved employees of the train companies are an essential part of the system. These train packers herd and push people onto the trains working to maximize the number of people who can fit.

For this activity, use two digital videos taken by Lyle Saxon, an Australian living and working in Japan. In the videos and associated blog postings, Saxon captures the flavor of train packing. The first video, from 1991, shows people boarding a train at the Hibarigaoka Station on the Seibu-Ikebukuro Line. The second video, from 2008 at the same station, shows that trains have become less crowded, thanks to additional train lines and the innovation of "flextime," allowing Japanese workers to arrive at work at hours of their own choosing, as long as they make up the time later.

TECHNOLOGY

Saxon (the creator of these Tokyo train videos) has blog postings that can be used, among other resources, to provide context. The address for the page containing links to the videos and providing his thoughts on them is www5d.biglobe.ne.jp/~LLLtrs/blog/prev/blog2008.html. Scroll down to the entry for 2008/07/21, "Tokyo Morning Trains (February 1991)."

FIGURE 1.4. YouTube video embedded on a teacher-created web page.

Figure 1.4 shows a YouTube video embedded on a teacher-created web page. Part of the reason for embedding the video is pedagogical. With an embedded video you can organize contextual information that will support the class discussion. For example, the 1991 video title mentions flextime. You might want to rename the video so that students do not have this information until they have viewed both videos.

FIGURE 1.5. YouTube video with highlighted embed code.

A second reason to embed videos rather than show them directly from YouTube is to control for inappropriate material. YouTube videos often come with comments, not all of which are appropriate for K–12 classrooms. The list of "Related Videos" may link to material that is highly objectionable. Accordingly, the best practice (almost always) is to place the video in a different page or to embed it in a slide show. The instructions are provided on the YouTube page itself (see Figure 1.5). For more information, see Chapter 6: "Acquiring Digital Video."

PEDAGOGY

Saxon's videos on Japanese trains can serve as an anticipatory set. In the setup, tell students they are about to see a video of people boarding a train, then show the first video. Provide some

> **BLOCKED SITES**
>
> Don't assume you will be able to acquire YouTube video clips at your school. Many school networks block YouTube and similar sites.

of the context immediately (e.g., this video was taken in 1991), but draw out the rest by posing questions to the students:

- Where do you think this video was recorded?

- What time of day is it?

- Where do you think the people are going?

- Is it a short trip or a long trip?

Other questions that may elicit student observations:

- Why do they do that?

- Why don't they wait for the next train?

- Don't people get angry?

- Why don't they just drive to work in cars?

Answers to these questions might include ideas such as:

- The train is fast and reliable, and they have to get to work on time.

- The next train will be just as crowded.

- Yes.

- They are more expensive to buy, operate, and park, and traffic jams can be just as unpleasant.

Students can record the questions, conduct research, and report back later, or you may want to post the questions to a blog or wiki page and have students answer them on their own over the course of the activity.

Once you have established the context of the first video, conduct a brief discussion around the question "What can be done to improve the situation?" Logical responses are to add more trains or otherwise provide alternative transportation routes. You may have to point out to students the costs of these alternatives. Adding new tracks may mean tearing down buildings, and in a densely populated city, doing so is not easy.

After students have explored the issue and discussed some possibilities, explain that they will now analyze another video, taken at the same station in 2008. Again, elicit observations. At first, students might not be able to detect any differences. They will likely notice that there are still large numbers of people cramming onto the trains. However, careful replaying should allow students to observe that the commuters do enter in a more orderly fashion, far fewer people are being pushed on at the end, and (tellingly) there are fewer packers. The driver of the train, in fact, is visible leaving the steering compartment and acting as a packer.

Once the class has discussed the second video and noted differences, ask students what might have changed in the 17 years between the two videos. Again, you can either provide the answer (the introduction of flextime) or have students research it themselves. An important part of this process is to help students expand the context of this video to include historical information. Such work might involve using population data from 1991 and 2008 or reviewing the political and economic situations at the two times.

You may also have students watch more videos by Saxon, many of which deal with Tokyo commuting and nightlife. If you wish to discuss Saxon as the author of the video, he makes a brief appearance in at least two of the other videos featured in his site.

To conclude the activity, ask students to review the videos and write answers to the following questions:

- What do these videos allow us to infer about the transportation system in Japan?

- What do these videos allow us to infer about Japanese culture?

- How did the policy of flextime change Japanese transportation and culture?

- What other information sources can help us analyze the Japanese transportation system and Japanese culture?

MORE IDEAS FOR ANALYZING DIGITAL VIDEO IN SOCIAL STUDIES

- Examine clips from presidential primary debates to explore the range of ideas within the Democratic and Republican parties. For example, the 2008 primaries featured a crowded field of candidates and multiple debates before producing party nominees. CNN hosted these debates and has made them available on its website (www.cnn.com/ELECTION/2008/debates). By studying the candidates and their stances on the issues, students can learn about the constituencies represented by each party and observe where their interests overlap and where they conflict.

- Analyze feature films to learn about history and its selective portrayal. James Percoco is a history teacher in Virginia and has written several books about his teaching practices. In *A Passion for the Past* (1998), Percoco describes how he uses *Glory* (1989), *Sergeant York* (1941), and other films to have students learn about the difference between "real history" and "reel history."

Creating Digital Video Activity

EARLY ELEMENTARY social studies instruction typically addresses topics such as families, holidays, and cultures. These topics can all come together in the discussion of the special meals featured at holidays. In November, for example, children can discuss both El Día de los Muertos (Day of the Dead), which is commonly celebrated in Mexico, and Thanksgiving, which is a traditional holiday in other North American countries, particularly Canada and the United States. Each holiday is observed with family gatherings, traditional customs, and special foods such as sugar skulls for Dia de los Muertos and pumpkin pie for Thanksgiving. Both holidays also have rich histories that reflect values and traditions in the places where they are celebrated.

You can use digital video to explain the cultural traditions associated with these holidays, showing students how the special foods are made and showing examples of families observing the holidays, and even showing historical examples of the holiday being celebrated. A topic as local, personal, and ubiquitous as holidays presents a unique opportunity to support students in creating their own digital videos about their families and the ways they observe the holidays.

This activity involves students' selecting a particular holiday or celebration, locating an image of the event, and constructing a digital video narrative about the event. Ideally, the photo should be a family photo. In this activity, students will describe the activities in the photo. If possible, the photo should show the student's family at a holiday occasion, preferably gathered around food or otherwise engaged in a traditional activity. The students will then provide a voice-over narration, describing the circumstances of the photo.

CONTENT STANDARDS

The Social Studies Standards are sponsored by the National Council for Social Studies, www.socialstudies.org/standards/strands/.

Families and Food
Social Studies—Culture
GRADE LEVELS: K-4

Objectives

- Students will understand that holidays and food are parts of cultural expression.

- Students will be able to use images to document or analyze a culture.

- Students will be able to construct a digital documentary from one or more images.

National Council for the Social Studies Thematic Strands Addressed

I   Culture

III   People, places, and environments

National Educational Technology Standards for Students (NETS·S) Addressed

1. **Creativity and Innovation**

   a.   apply existing knowledge to generate new ideas, products, or processes

   b.   create original works as a means of personal or group expression

2. **Communication and Collaboration**

   a.   interact, collaborate, and publish with peers, experts, or others employing a variety of digital environments and media

   b.   communicate information and ideas effectively to multiple audiences using a variety of media and formats

   c.   develop cultural understanding and global awareness by engaging with learners of other cultures

   d.   contribute to project teams to produce original works or solve problems

3. **Research and Information Fluency**

   b.   locate, organize, analyze, evaluate, synthesize, and ethically use information from a variety of sources and media

4. **Critical Thinking, Problem Solving, and Decision Making**

   a.   identify and define authentic problems and significant questions for investigation

   b.   plan and manage activities to develop a solution or complete a project

6. **Technology Operations and Concepts**

   a.   understand and use technology systems

   b.   select and use applications effectively and productively

Technology/Materials Needed

- Windows Photo Story 3 (for PC users) or iMovie (for Mac users)
- Options for completing the project on the web: PrimaryAccess (www.primaryaccess.org) or VoiceThread (http://voicethread.com)

CONTENT

This lesson will allow you to branch off into many different directions, such as family structure, holidays, and culture. For example, you may want to study the cultural importance and timing of holidays such as Halloween and Diwali. These holidays often occur at the same time of the year, but because Halloween is a North American and European holiday and Diwali is a South Asian holiday, various calendars will place the holidays on different days each year. The lunisolar Hindu calendar is commonly used in South Asia and is used to mark Diwali. Halloween is dated according to the solar Gregorian calendar.

You can find plenty of other examples when important holidays do not align. For example, on some years, Chinese New Year will fall in January on the Gregorian calendar and not February and, thus, be within a few weeks of the Western New Year's Day on January 1. As another example, the Muslim holy month of Ramadan falls near the Christian holiday of Easter in some years and the Jewish observance of Yom Kippur in other years. By comparing across holidays, particularly familiar and unfamiliar holidays, you will be able to broaden students' cultural perspectives and demonstrate the universal nature of some cultural practices.

TECHNOLOGY

When working with young students, simplicity is the key. Maintaining a simple focus will help prevent the technology from overwhelming the content. You may even complete much of the technology work, but leave portions as students' hands-on work. In all cases, you will be able to focus on the content and pedagogy more if you keep the technological aspects simple.

For creating the video, Windows Photo Story 3 is an excellent choice for PC users. The narration can be recorded with one visual at a time and utilizing appropriate pans and zooms. For example, if a video is describing a Thanksgiving dinner, you may want to include one copy of the image to focus on groups of family members, one to show main courses, one to show desserts, and so forth.

A good choice for Mac users is iMovie. Be sure to load the required photos into the library before trying to access them from iMovie. You may also want to include multiple copies of the image(s) to allow pans and zooms to highlight different aspects of the photograph.

PrimaryAccess (www.primaryaccess.org) and VoiceThread (http://voicethread.com) are options for completing the project on the web. Both of these online tools host the working

materials on the web, meaning students and
teachers can work from anywhere without
having to move files from computer to computer.

In some situations, it will be easier for you to
handle loading the images into the editing
program or website instead of the students.
Once the photos are loaded, students can record
the statements they have written. You can then
either fine-tune the timing and motion yourself
or allow students to do it. In our experience,
Photo Story and Voice Thread are easier for young students to handle than iMovie.

> **SHARING VIDEOS**
>
> Learn more about sharing
> videos in Chapter 8:
> "Communicating with
> Digital Video."

Once the projects are finished, save them as movie files and share! Digital video files
can be linked to a teacher web page or uploaded to a channel on YouTube or TeacherTube
(teachertube.com).

PEDAGOGY

A number of pedagogical questions will need to be addressed as you adapt this digital
video activity for your class. For example, what time of the year is the best to introduce these concepts? In the United States, many holidays fall in October (Halloween),
November (Veterans Day, Thanksgiving), and December (Christmas, Hanukkah,
Kwanzaa). This lesson can be conducted at any point during the year or can even be
revisited at multiple points throughout the year. In any case, bring it up in advance of a
holiday. For example, to take advantage of children's excitement about Valentine's Day,
initiate this activity at the end of January or the beginning of February.

As you consider which holidays to address, you should also consider your classroom and
your community. Which cultural traditions do you think will be represented among your
students? What cultural groups are present in your community that might be willing to
demonstrate traditional practices for your students? Of course, you will also want to be
sensitive to students and families who might not want to fully participate in the activity.
For some families, holidays can even be a painful time of year, reminding them of loss
or separation. Try to anticipate where problems might arise and speak to students and
parents privately.

When teaching this activity, your tasks are twofold. First, introduce the content. The
content (holidays, families, cultures, food, and in-depth topics such as calendars) can be
introduced through a variety of means. One approach is to read aloud and then discuss a
relevant children's book, such as *Behind the Mask*, written and illustrated by Yangsook
Choi, which is a story about Halloween and a traditional Korean folk dance called
Talchum. Another approach might be to lead a discussion with the students about their
families' practices during the holiday.

Once children have an understanding of the topic, your second task is to introduce and facilitate the digital video-making activity. Perhaps the best tactic is to show them a sample video you have created yourself. A sample video can both provide a model of a finished product and set the tone for sharing and making students feel more comfortable about sharing. Once students have viewed and discussed the model, explain that they will be making their own video.

To make the video, students will first locate appropriate photos. Invite students to bring in one—or two—but not more! family photos showing their family, food, and activities during a holiday. If students bring in print photos, you can scan them or take a picture with a digital camera to produce digital versions.

DIGITAL IMAGES

If you need to find additional photos to illustrate foods or activities, try www.flickr.com/creativecommons, searching for photos that allow users to make derivative works.

After the photos are collected, students should write short statements about what is happening in the photos. Depending on the content focus of your lesson, make sure that students include information that extends what they already know about the topic to include something new they have learned. For example, if the focus is on calendars, students can comment on where the holiday falls on the calendar, how that date was determined, how holiday dates might change over consecutive years, or how the holiday might fall on different days in different calendars.

The key here is to support students with clear expectations about what they should include in their voice-over narrative. As you scaffold the activity, provide students with the beginnings of sentences that they then fill in, such as "This is my family at…. Present are…. We are eating…. We are doing…." These statements will be read out loud to form the voice-over narration, so be sure they are clearly written and rehearsed. If the videos will be posted on the Internet, remind them to limit the amount of personal information in the final version!

MORE IDEAS FOR CREATING DIGITAL VIDEO IN SOCIAL STUDIES

■ Students can document landmarks in their neighborhoods or communities and construct movies explaining the cultural significance of these sites.

■ Students can collect images from online archives and use them to create digital documentaries. For example, students studying Japanese-American history could use the Library of Congress' collection of photographs taken at the Manzanar Relocation Camp to compose a documentary about internment.

▪ Students can interview family members of people in the community about their memories of historical events and use these as source material for a classroom inquiry on history and remembrance. Example questions might be "What do you recall about the energy crisis of the 1970s?" or "What do you recall about the American invasions of Grenada and Panama in the 1980s and 1990s?"

Conclusion

THE ACTIVITIES described here are only a small sample of the full range of possibilities for applying digital video to social studies instruction. Digital video can allow you to enhance or compress content, as well as engage students in critical thinking. We have presented these activities to illustrate how students can watch, analyze, and create digital videos. These teacher and student actions require different pedagogical approaches and emerge from different educational aims. In order to best use digital video in your class, stay focused on your aims and the approaches that will support those aims. The activities also draw upon a range of technologies, from simple tools to more complex ones. It is important not to let the use of more complex digital video obstruct your instructional goals.

As you design your own activities with digital video, keep in mind the options available to you and observe the ways in which the technology interacts with the content and pedagogy to make your instruction more powerful.

References

Dimitriadis, G. (2000). "Making history go" at a local community center: Popular media and the construction of historical knowledge among African American youth. *Theory and Research in Social Education, 28*(1), 40-64.

International Society for Technology in Education. (2007). *National educational technology standards for students* (2nd ed.). Eugene, OR: Author.

Mayer, R. E. (2005). Cognitive theory of multimedia learning. In R. E. Mayer (Ed.), *The Cambridge handbook of multimedia learning* (pp. 31-48). New York, NY: Cambridge University Press.

National Council for Social Studies (NCSS). (1994). *Expectations of excellence: Curriculum standards for social studies.* Washington, DC: Author.

Ogburn, W. F. (1934). *You and machines.* Chicago, IL: University of Chicago Press.

Percoco, J. (1998). *A passion for the past.* Portsmouth, NH: Heinemann.

Vanden, H. (2007). Bringing Latin America to life with films in the classroom. *Social Education, 71*(4), 177-181.

CHAPTER 2

Margaret L. Niess and
Janet M. Walker*

digital video in mathematics education

MATHEMATICS IS typically described as a body of knowledge about quantity, structure, space, and change. Some people consider mathematics to be the language of science. Some conceive it as a way of thinking that results in organizing, analyzing, and synthesizing data. Some describe mathematics as a study of patterns, while still others envision mathematics as an art. Irrespective of these various viewpoints, mathematics is a discipline that has significantly advanced through the use of digital technologies with computational, graphical, and symbolic capabilities.

High-speed, technological advancements in the quality of image display, color, and smooth motion have paved the way for amazing digital video representations for mathematical developments such as in fractal and chaos theories. A quick Internet search reveals

TEACHING WITH DIGITAL VIDEO

39

numerous displays of digital videos characterizing the structure, patterns, and art of mathematics.

If you try searching the word *fractals* at the popular website YouTube, you will find fascinating videos. In the video *Fractal Zoom Mandelbrot Corner* (www.youtube.com/watch?v=G_GBwuYuOOs), the camera zooms in on the famous Mandelbrot fractal. As the view of the fractal is enlarged, the similarity of the parts of the object to the overall image is quickly obvious. This image was developed using iterations (a form of feedback called recursion). The result is a marvelous mathematical expression in an artful pattern.

Advanced digital technologies have changed the nature of today's culture as well as the way mathematicians think about and do mathematics. Have these technologies also changed how students today are learning mathematics—are they using today's technologies in learning mathematical ideas?

Before answering this question, consider the students in your school. The majority are exposed to and engaged in a culture where many hours are spent texting, playing video games, and "talking" on social networking sites such as MySpace or Facebook, often while watching television. Many newer communication technologies require and facilitate interaction. Students with cell phones rarely pass written notes to each other; instead, they text messages in an abbreviated language. Over the past few decades, with the advancement of digital technologies, our society has moved from communicating with others over the telephone, by mail, or in person to communicating by e-mails and instant messages that may even be in digital video format. These technologies have changed the way many adolescents (and even adults) interact with each other, suggesting new ways they can interact and learn both inside and outside the classroom.

Let's return to the question of students learning mathematics with today's digital technologies. In 2000, the National Council of Teachers of Mathematics (NCTM) published a Technology Principle in its *Principles and Standards for School Mathematics* stating, "The existence, versatility, and power of technology make it possible and necessary to reexamine what mathematics students should learn as well as how they can best learn it" (NCTM, 2000, p. 25).

Many digital technologies have been considered useful for students in learning mathematics: graphing calculators, applets of virtual manipulatives (such as those available through the National Library of Virtual Manipulatives at http://nlvm.usu.edu/en/nav/vLibrary.html), spreadsheets, and dynamic geometry tools (such as Geometer's Sketchpad). Each of these technologies provides visual representations, enabling students to explore mathematical ideas in more dynamic ways. When asked to identify technologies for teaching mathematics, Joe Garofalo, a mathematics teacher education professor from the University of Virginia, proposed a technology that surprised many of the participants at his 2006 workshop: "iPods—because students have them and we as teachers need to think of how this technology can be useful in teaching mathematics."

Many of today's school-aged youth actively contribute to YouTube, where they upload, view, and share their video clips as a way of communicating their thinking and ideas. They use simple digital video tools such as cell phones, digital cameras with movie settings, and inexpensive camcorders to create and share video, communicating with others far beyond their local community.

In such an environment, students should no longer be expected to learn mathematical concepts and processes only by sitting and listening to long explanations. They can be more actively involved in constructing their knowledge with the aid of digital video as they explore the amazing world of mathematics. Teachers of mathematics must consider how they can adapt their teaching, incorporating these technologies to help students learn mathematics in ways similar to how they learn and communicate outside the classroom. This chapter challenges you to incorporate digital videos in ways that provide exciting and effective mathematics learning opportunities for your students.

The perspective we present goes beyond the traditional view of videos as being made by others and passively watched by students. We suggest ways digital videos can be used to present challenging mathematical questions for students. Watching, analyzing, and creating are three lenses we use for describing active student engagement with video. Many videos can also be layered with other dynamic, interactive media to engage today's students in thinking about mathematics in ways that were previously difficult to achieve.

Visualization is an important tool in problem solving, and students need multiple visualization opportunities if this tool is to be developed (NCTM, 2000). Through watching appropriate digital videos, students can further develop their visualization skills. Watching is a strategy that requires gathering and integrating information from multiple sources, both audio and visual.

For example, students can make a conjecture about the mathematical notion of similarity through this simple video activity: Students watch multiple images captured using a zoom-in and zoom-out feature in a simple video editor, such as iMovie or Windows Movie Maker. As they watch, they should consider whether the images presented in various sizes are similar. To determine if the images are similar or perhaps even congruent, they can collect data on the primary features of the images that appear to be similar. Entering the data in a spreadsheet table allows students to explore the ratio of the measurements for each feature. Does a common ratio exist for all features? If it does, what does that mean?

Reasoning is also a fundamental part of mathematics, and reasoning mathematically is a habit of mind that must be developed through consistent use and in a variety of contexts

(NCTM, 2000). Analysis is a reasoning process that means "separation of a whole into its component parts" (Analysis, 2010).

The movie *The Sound of Music* received the Academy Award for Best Picture in 1965 and was nominated for an award for its art direction. You can devise a mathematical problem by separating or distinguishing the component parts of the various scenes in *The Sound of Music* to discover how these parts helped create a movie recognized for outstanding art direction. Engage students in analyzing clips of the poses used in the song and dance numbers, such as when the children are singing "Do-Re-Mi" with Maria. Why are only six of the children shown in the scene where they follow Maria across a meadow while singing? What happened to little Gretl? Probably, the choreographer purposefully chose to maintain symmetry in the scene. Analyze the geometry in clips throughout the movie and make a conjecture about why the visual effects were so pleasing. What geometric concepts were used in creating these visual effects? You may find Geometer's Sketchpad and spreadsheet capabilities to be useful in this analysis.

Communication is an essential aspect of mathematics. According to NCTM's *Principles and Standards for School Mathematics* (2000), communication is a way of sharing ideas and clarifying understanding. Creating videos is another experience with potential for helping students communicate their mathematical understandings. Students can create a video of someone walking in front of a camera in the movement that describes a particular function. For example, if you ask a student to move in front of the camera in the shape of the function $y = abs(x)$, the student should start about 3 meters away from the camera, walk toward the camera at a constant rate, and then walk away from the camera at the same constant rate. A student can be video recorded moving in front of the camera, and other students can try to figure out the path of that person. They can find the solution either by graphing the movement or by defining it as a function, which they demonstrate by entering the data in their graphing calculators or spreadsheets and displaying both the tabular and graphical representations. Students can include these visuals in their video creations to display the multiple representations of the person's movement.

The challenge for mathematics teachers is to take advantage of technologies, such as digital video, and integrate them actively and consistently in meaningful ways in mathematics instruction. John Keller's (1987) attention, relevance, confidence, and satisfaction (ARCS) instructional model provides a valuable model for teaching with images. Images, whether still or active, can be used to show concrete examples of concepts such as polynomial multiplication, polynomials factoring, slope, rates, measurement, three-dimensional objects, and even mathematics in nature and art. Images can be used to draw students' attention to a concept by making it relevant to their interests. Dynamic, interactive technologies are available to assist students in making conjectures about the patterns they are viewing.

Students can explore mathematical concepts and processes in visual ways and use digital video as a tool for communicating their thinking. Video media provide capabilities that engage them in higher order thinking in a classroom where traditionally they have been expected to follow a set of rules for solving a problem. With students' confidence in using the multimedia technologies, they also gain confidence in learning mathematics with the technologies. Your charge is to determine effective ways for integrating video technologies with other technology tools that students use as they explore mathematics.

In this chapter we describe ways for video technologies to be integrated, layered, and incorporated with other dynamic technologies for enhancing students' mathematics learning. The instructional key is to engage students in thinking about ideas presented with moving images and make connections with mathematical ideas. Of course, whenever you incorporate digital video and other technology, your goal must always be to facilitate students' mathematical understandings. Students need the guidance of a skillful teacher who understands what they know and how they learn (NCTM, 2000).

Watching Digital Video Activities

WATCHING IS an obvious activity with videos, but the mathematics curriculum is packed with content, leaving teachers little time for engaging students in watching 30- to 40-minute videos, much less full-length movies. On the other hand, video clips (short excerpts from movies, television shows, professionally prepared educational videos, or personally created videos) can quickly engage students in mathematical exploration. Video clips can be used to introduce new mathematical concepts and processes; illustrate mathematics in nature, art, or other contexts in the real world; and engage students in expressing their mathematical understandings as they think about what has been said or displayed.

For example, you might introduce chaos theory with a short clip from *Jurassic Park*. In *Austin Powers: The Spy Who Shagged Me*, Dr. Evil's clone, whom he named "Mini-Me," is "one-eighth the size" of Dr. Evil. Use a video clip from this movie to introduce and discuss transformations, specifically dilations. See how engaging students in watching videos provides a useful instructional tool for engaging students in thinking about mathematics.

You can find many more ideas for using the watching mode in a mathematics class at these websites:

- Math Bits–http://mathbits.com/MathBits/MathMovies/MathMovies.htm

- PBS Mathline–www.pbs.org/teachers/mathline/concepts/movies.shtm

- Math Education Free Videos–
  http://iae-pedia.org/Math_Education_Free_Videos

If you are thinking about using videos in a watching mode, be sure to preview every video clip to ensure that the content is appropriate for the age group you are teaching. Select a short, relevant clip for the content of the day. The best clips used in this watching mode are 1 to 5 minutes in length. Make sure the video or media player is ready before class begins, queuing it to the location of the clip you want to show. Set the stage for the video so that students don't assume it is merely padding to keep them occupied until you are ready to begin "teaching." Students must engage in more than *passive* watching. Provide a mathematical challenge that requires students to watch in preparation for responding after the video. Variety in the mathematics classroom helps to maintain students' interest, but be careful about overusing video clips.

This section provides detailed discussions for using video clips from *Abbott and Costello: In the Navy* and *Alice in Wonderland.* You can extend beyond these ideas to find other ways in which watching might aid in the development of concepts and processes in the mathematics classroom. Explore how these activities engage students in watching, listening to, and exploring mathematical ideas. Consider how students might use different technologies, such as calculators, Geometer's Sketchpad, and spreadsheets, as they think about and explore what they have observed in the video. Remember the importance of multiple representations of mathematical ideas and of guiding students in communicating their mathematical thinking in ways that deepen their understanding of mathematics.

Abbott and Costello Argue about Addition, Multiplication, and Division
Mathematics–Place Value
GRADE LEVELS: 4–8

Objectives

- Students use place value concepts in explaining relationships among operations of addition, multiplication, and division.

- Students select appropriate methods for explaining and justifying their thinking about the use of place value implications in addition, multiplication, and division.

- Students make and investigate mathematical conjectures and arguments with respect to place value and the operations of addition, multiplication, and division.

National Council of Teachers of Mathematics (NCTM) Content Standards Addressed

- Understand meanings of operations of addition, multiplication and division (NCTM, Number and Operations Standard, Grades 3–5)

- Develop fluency in adding, multiplying, and dividing whole number (NCTM, Number and Operations Standard, Grades 3–5)

- Develop and use strategies to estimate the results of whole-number computations and to judge the reasonableness of such results (NCTM, Number and Operations Standards, Grades 3–5)

- Communicate mathematical thinking coherently and clearly to peers and teachers (NCTM, Communication Standard, Grades 3–5)

National Educational Technology Standards for Students (NETS·S) Addressed

1. **Creativity and Innovation**

    a. apply existing knowledge to generate new ideas, products, or processes

2. **Communication and Collaboration**

    d. contribute to project teams to produce original works or solve problems

4. **Critical Thinking, Problem Solving, and Decision Making**

    a. identify and define authentic problems and significant questions for investigation

    d. use multiple processes and diverse perspectives to explore alternative solutions

Technology/Materials Needed

- Video clip from YouTube called Abbott and Costello 13 X 7 is 28: www.youtube.com/watch?v=Lo4NCXOX0p8

CONTENT

YouTube is a rich resource for video clips and short movies you can use to challenge students to watch carefully and engage in mathematical thinking. Consider, for example, Abbott and Costello's 1941 movie *In the Navy*. This video has a scene where Lou Costello is explaining to Bud Abbott that he has 28 donuts to share among 7 people. Lou decides that to share the donuts fairly and equally each person should get 13. Bud questions Lou's mathematics, and the scene progresses until Bud gives up trying to convince Lou that his arithmetic is wrong.

This video clip portraying Abbott and Costello and their different understandings of 28 divided by 7 is an excellent example of a video that can be used in the elementary grades. Students in upper elementary grades need to be able to compute fluently and make reasonable estimates. In order to achieve these actions, they must have a solid understanding of place-value structure of the base-10 number system. Their knowledge of the operations of multiplication and division relies heavily on their place-value understandings. Communication is a tool that can be used to engage students in developing a deeper understanding rather than mere memorization of multiplication and division rules. Engage students in mathematical discourse about their strategies for estimating the results of problems requiring these operations.

Through their discussions, the students expand their understanding of the place-value structure and its impact on multiplication and division computations. Conversations that engage students in explaining the processes involved in the different computations help them organize their thinking and deepen their mathematical understanding. Watching and listening to the ways in which others, such as Lou Costello, solve specific computational problems engages them in making mathematical sense of underlying multiplication and division operations.

TECHNOLOGY

You can play the video from the YouTube website on your computer. To eliminate potentially inappropriate material surrounding the video, you may also embed the clip in your own website by inserting the embedded code provided on the YouTube video page. Another option is to capture the video and watch it offline (follow the instructions in Chapter 6: "Acquiring Digital Video").

PEDAGOGY

Begin the class by posing the following problem to the students: "How can 28 donuts be shared equally among 7 people?"

Have students share their explanations for different ways of thinking about the problem. One student might draw seven boxes on the board and draw a circle for each donut on a tray (showing 28 donuts). Then, as she places a donut in a box (gives it to a person), she erases a donut from the tray. The process results in each person receiving four donuts. Another student might suggest that the problem is a division problem and explain that 28 divided by 7 is 4, since 4 times 7 is 28. Still another person might draw on the board seven groups, each containing four marks, and then count the marks up to 28. Encourage different communication strategies as well as thinking about the relationships among repeated addition, multiplication, and division.

Introduce the students to the two people in the movie—Bud Abbott and Lou Costello—showing pictures of the two men (the YouTube website contains many images). Describe them as comedians who often have disagreements about arithmetic. In fact, the same donut problem your class just completed is one of the problems about which Abbott and Costello disagreed on the solution. Instruct the students that they will watch the clip to identify which one of the two comedians actually understands the arithmetic of the problem. Show the 3-minute video clip of Abbott and Costello discussing the number of donuts 7 people would get if there were 28 donuts in total.

After watching this clip, ask students, "Can the quotient possibly be 13? What procedure does Costello use to show that 28 divided by 7 is 13?" You may want to show the video a second time to remind the students about the various ways that Abbott and Costello consider the problem: division of 28 by 7; proving the division correct through multiplication of 7 times 4; supplying another proof of the correctness of the division with repeated addition by adding seven 13s. Stop the video and replay parts as needed to make sure the students have identified the arithmetic solutions and proofs.

Discuss Lou Costello's division method. Does this method work for all division problems? Ask the students to consider a similar problem: 18 donuts to be shared equally by 3 people. Have them try Costello's method for 18 divided by 3. Does this result make sense? How can each person be given 24 donuts when there are only 18 donuts in the beginning? Why is Costello's division method wrong? Add to this discussion the "proofs" that Costello used to verify his result (multiplication and repeated addition). Why are these proofs incorrect? Encourage the students to talk about the meaning of place-value as the basic structure in the base-10 number system.

Organize the students in three different groups to develop explanations they might use to help Costello see and understand that his ways of doing the operations are incorrect. Challenge the first group to respond to the question about Costello's way of dividing. Why is his method incorrect? Ask the second group to develop an explanation of why the multiplication proof is incorrect and the third group to develop an explanation of why the repeated addition is incorrect.

Encourage the groups to communicate their explanations in creative ways. They might develop a play and act it out for the class, create a video to communicate their explanations, or draw visuals to explain.

After the groups share their explanations, discuss the importance of communication in mathematics. Communication is a way of talking about mathematics, a way that "helps build meaning and permanence of ideas" (NCTM, 2000, p. 60). Yes, this process does take time. Students' experiences in communicating their personal understandings and explanations require them to think deeply about the operations and how the ideas are related to each other.

MODIFICATIONS

Provide multiple representations by adding other technologies along with this video clip. If 28 divided by 7 is 13, then what should 7 times 13 be? Have students demonstrate this product with handheld base-10 blocks. Use the Rectangle Multiplication virtual manipulative download from the National Library of Virtual Manipulatives (http://nlvm.usu.edu/en/nav/frames_asid_192_g_2_t_1.html) to demonstrate that 7 times 13 is 91 and not 28, as Costello claims (see Figure 2.1). Change the sliders to find the product of 13 times 7 and discuss the commutative nature of multiplication. Have students use their handheld blocks to verify the sums, products, and quotients in the video.

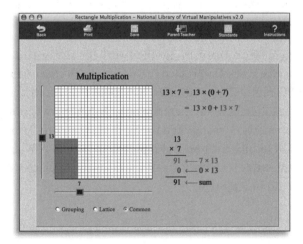

FIGURE 2.1. Virtual manipulative for demonstrating products of numbers (Rectangle Multiplication available from http://nlvm.usu.edu/en/nav/frames_asid_192_g_2_t_1.html).

Vary the context with a different clip. A similar clip on YouTube called *Ma and Pa Kettle Find Uranium* provides another look at the same problem Abbott and Costello had. This 3½-minute video can be found at www.youtube.com/watch?v=zlXtCVaC9ns.

Vary the problem. In another Abbott and Costello video, the two are exchanging money. *Two Tens for a Five* is an approximately 1-minute portion of a longer video clip (*Abbott & Costello: "Two Tens for a Five" & "Who's on First"*) found at www.youtube.com/watch?v=V1fJDIXEq9w. Focus only on this portion of the video and have the students determine how much each person has after each exchange of money. After watching the video, ask the students which of the exchanges were correct and which were incorrect. Again, you will probably need to replay the video as you help the students gather the data they need to respond. Students can be asked questions about this clip such as, "If Abbott starts with five 10-dollar bills, what does he have left after the skit? If Costello starts with ten 5-dollar bills, what does he have left?" Students can be asked to create a similar silly skit but with other mathematics concepts, such as time, fractions, or algebra.

Vary the video. *Donald in Mathmagicland* is an entertaining example of Donald Duck learning to play billiards based on mathematics (www.math.harvard.edu/~knill/mathmovies/swf/donald.html). Challenge students to learn how to do some activity that is mathematical (but not obviously mathematical) and explain how mathematics is used in it. Students might choose a sport, dance choreography, theatre production, or music.

> ## CONTENT STANDARDS
>
> The Principles and Standards for School Mathematics are sponsored by the National Council of Teachers of Mathematics, http://standards.nctm.org.

Alice in Wonderland
Mathematics–Scaling
GRADE LEVELS: 4–8

Objectives

- Students use ratios to dilate or shrink an object.

- Students determine the ratio of dilation from a given transformation.

- Students determine how the area or perimeter of a polygon might change as the figure is dilated.

National Council of Teachers of Mathematics (NCTM) Content Standards Addressed

- Understand measurable attributes of objectives and the units, systems, and processes of measurement (NCTM, Measurement expectations, Grades 6–8)

- Understand numbers, ways of representing numbers, relationships among numbers, and number systems—understand and use ratios and proportions to represent quantitative relationships (NCTM, Number and Operations expectations, Grades 6–8)

- Apply appropriate techniques, tools, and formulas to determine measurements (NCTM, Measurement expectations, Grades 6–8)

National Educational Technology Standards for Students (NETS·S) Addressed

1. **Creativity and Innovation**

   a. apply existing knowledge to generate new ideas, products, or processes

   b. create original works as a means of personal or group expression

   c. use models and simulations to explore complex systems and issues

   d. identify trends and forecast possibilities

2. **Communication and Collaboration**

   d. contribute to project teams to produce original works or solve problems

3. **Research and Information Fluency**

   d. process data and report results

4. **Critical Thinking, Problem Solving, and Decision Making**

   c. collect and analyze data to identify solutions and/or make informed decisions

   d. use multiple processes and diverse perspectives to explore alternative solutions

6. **Technology Operations and Concepts**

   d. transfer current knowledge to learning of new technologies

Technology/Materials Needed

- Download of the Transformations–Dilation virtual manipulative from the National Library of Virtual Manipulatives (http://nlvm.usu.edu/en/nav/frames_asid_295_g_3_t_3.html)

- Video of *Alice in Wonderland* (if using the 1999 remake, queue it to the first scene about 5 minutes 30 seconds into the movie; students watch about 8 minutes of the video).

- Calculators or spreadsheet

CONTENT

Another video clip students can watch in the mathematics classroom comes from the movie *Alice in Wonderland* (the 1999 remake, the 2010 remake, or the 1951 original). In the opening scene, Alice sees a white rabbit and follows it down the rabbit hole. She enters a long hallway with a gold key on the table. She proceeds around a curtain with a small door behind it and uses the key to unlock the door. She sees a beautiful garden through the door, but cannot fit through the door herself. She finds a small bottle labeled "DRINK ME," and the drink shrinks her to the right size to fit through the door. After a few minutes she realizes that she left the key on the table, but she is too small to reach it. She panics and proceeds to eat a cake that says "EAT ME," which makes her grow to 9-feet tall. The story continues.

This activity is an excellent opening segment for a unit on transformations, specifically dilations. Students can see how Alice shrinks and then grows, thus giving them an intuitive sense of what it means to dilate or shrink an object. Furthermore, students can explore how they might change as a result of shrinking or growing as Alice did. The activity can then be expanded to determine how polygons might change with respect to dilation and how the length of the sides and area change with that dilation.

PEDAGOGY

Use the Transformations-Dilation virtual manipulative to introduce the idea of scaling (as in Figures 2.2A and 2.2B). The scale slider can be moved to create a similar figure that is 0.44 the scale of the larger object or even 2.0 times the scale of the original figure. Ask students what they observe about the figure as the scale changes. Talk about the different features of the image. Are the two figures exactly the same? What happens when the scale is changed? Are the images still similar? Students should describe how they are the same and how they are different.

Ask, "Who has read the book or seen the movie *Alice in Wonderland?*" Allow students to share what they remember about the story. If not many students are familiar with the plot, give them a quick synopsis so that they have a context. Tell them they will watch a few minutes of the movie and must pay close attention to Alice and how she shrinks and grows in the movie. Run the clip for about 8 minutes until Alice shrinks and floats away in the pool of her own tears.

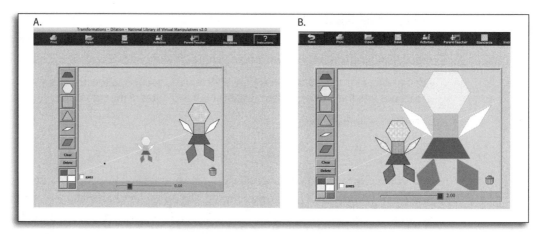

FIGURE 2.2A and **2.2B**. Resizing a figure with a scale factor change from 0.44 to 2.0 (Transformations-Dilation from the National Library of Virtual Manipulatives, http://nlvm.usu.edu/en/nav/frames_asid_295_g_3_t_3.html).

After stopping the video, ask students to summarize what happened to Alice as she drank the potion and then as she ate the cake. "How much did Alice have to shrink to fit through the small door, and how much would she need to grow to be able to reach the key on the table?" Suggest that the students model Alice's changes with the Transformations-Dilation virtual manipulative.

Ask students if this action can be modeled using mathematics. Connect the problem in the video to the classroom. How would Alice look in the classroom if she shrank to one-eighth of her size? Assuming that Alice was an average sized young woman of 5' 4", how tall would she be after shrinking? Discuss what conjectures students might make about each of these challenges. Students should consider the following questions:

- Measure the height of your desks. Would Alice be as tall as your desk if she were one-eighth her size?

- If you were shrunk down to one-eighth your size, how tall would you be? What would be the length of your hand? What size shoe would you wear? Would you be as tall as the desk? What object in the classroom would be the same height as you?

- After Alice ate the cake, she was 9 feet tall. Could she walk through the classroom doorway without stooping? What ratio did she grow from her original height (using the average height)? What ratio did she grow from her shrunken version?

◇	A	B	C	D	E	F	G
1	Alice in Wonderland						
2					Alice		
3	Changing Alice by	1/8					
4							
5					Changing Alice by	1/8	
6	Feet	Inches	Total inches		Total inches	Feet	Inches
7	5	4	64		8	0	8
8							
9					Desk		
10	Feet	Inches	Total inches		Total inches	Feet	Inches
11	2	1	25		3.125	0	3.125

FIGURE 2.3. Spreadsheet prepared for considering Alice when she is shrunk to one-eighth her original size.

Investigate these challenges using a spreadsheet (see Figure 2.3). Use the spreadsheet functions to do the following:

- change feet and inches to just inches

- find 1/8 of the inches

- convert the inches back to feet and inches

MODIFICATIONS

Vary the ratio for shrinking Alice. With a middle school class, it might be useful to start with a simpler ratio such as one-fourth. With a more advanced group of students, consider a ratio such as 2/5 or even 11/17.

Extend the mathematical ideas to the notion of limits. This scene has another mathematical connotation to it. As Alice is drinking the liquid in the small bottle, she wonders what size she would end up being if she drank more of it and whether, perhaps, she would end up "going out altogether, like a candle." If Alice continues to drink the liquid and continues to shrink to one-eighth her size, can she "go out altogether?" Have students display the decreasing size in a spreadsheet both in a table and in a graph. Discuss the concept of a limit as they explain the changes in size.

Create scale models of items that Alice might see. Ask students to think of the items in Alice's world. Challenge students to create a scale version of a church, a courthouse, or a car that might exist in Alice's world if she were 25 inches tall.

Consider other mathematical features in Alice's world. It is believed that because Lewis Carroll was an Oxford University mathematician, he included many references to mathematics in his works. In Alice in Wonderland, Chapter 2: "Pool of Tears," Alice tries to perform multiplication, but it seems that she is doing this operation in different bases. She states, "Let me see: four times five is twelve, and four times six is thirteen, and four times seven is—oh dear! I shall never get to twenty at that rate!" ($4 \times 5 = 12$ in base 18, $4 \times 6 = 13$ in base 21, and 4×7 could be 14 in base 24).

Analyzing Digital Video Activities

ANALYSIS IS at the heart of reasoning in mathematics. In mathematics, people analyze situations and models to define functions describing relationships. Students need experiences that guide them as they learn to reason mathematically. They need opportunities to make conjectures based on their analysis and to communicate the thinking that directs them toward these conjectures. Engaging students in analysis of events in video clips is one way of providing these important experiences. In a classroom, students might watch video clips of people dancing, riding bikes, or traveling in cars and then analyze the motions they are seeing. What patterns do they see in the dance routines? How fast is a car going in a video? These types of activities can be used to interject analysis into video-recorded experiences.

The Path of a Rock Embedded in a Tire
Mathematics–Cycloids
GRADE LEVELS: 9–12

Objectives

- Students describe nonlinear relationships.

- Students use graphical and tabular representations to visualize a mathematical situation.

- Students define the nonlinear function of a cycloid.

National Council of Teachers of Mathematics (NCTM) Content Standards Addressed

- Represent and analyze mathematical situations and structures using algebraic symbols (NCTM, Algebra Standard Grades 9–12)

- Analyze change in various contexts—changing from graphical and numerical data (NCTM, Algebra Standard Grades 9–12)

- Use visualization, spatial reasoning, and geometric modeling to solve problems (NCTM, Geometry Standard Grades 9–12)

National Educational Technology Standards for Students (NETS·S) Addressed

1. **Creativity and Innovation**

   a. apply existing knowledge to generate new ideas, products, or processes

   c. use models and simulations to explore complex systems and issues

   d. identify trends and forecast possibilities

2. **Communication and Collaboration**

   b. communicate information and ideas effectively to multiple audiences using a variety of media and formats

   d. contribute to project teams to produce original works or solve problems

3. **Research and Information Fluency**

   a. plan strategies to guide inquiry

   b. locate, organize, analyze, evaluate, synthesize, and ethically use information from a variety of sources and media

   d. process data and report results

4. **Critical Thinking, Problem Solving, and Decision Making**

   a. identify and define authentic problems and significant questions for investigation

   c. collect and analyze data to identify solutions and make informed decisions

6. **Technology Operations and Concepts**

   a.   understand and use technology systems

   b.   select and use applications effectively and productively

Technology/Materials Needed

■   Before class, download the *Bicycle Rock—Part 1* video from the Screening Room at http://site.aace. org/video/books/teaching/math (or create a video of your own showing person riding a bike with a rock embedded in the tire). Note that in our video, the rock is visible and the clicking sound is audible.

■   *Bicycle Rock—Part 2* (found at http://site.aace.org/video/books/teaching/math) highlights the path of the rock as Abby rides her bike.

■   You may also want to set up a demonstration bike in the classroom. Place it in an inverted position to display the rock in the tire similar to the *Inverted Bicycle* video in the SITE Screening Room at http://site.aace.org/video/books/teaching/math.

■   Wheel analysis videos demonstrating the relationship of the height of the rock from the center of the tire versus the distance the tire travels:

   ■   *Wheel with Numbers*—Found at http://site.aace.org/video/books/teaching/math/

   ■   *Wheel with Graph*—Found at http://site.aace.org/video/books/teaching/math/

■   Cycloid video from Jim Wilson, University of Georgia. This video simulates the path of a rock embedded in a tire: http://jwilson.coe.uga.edu/EMT668/EMT668.Student.Folders/ BrombacherAarnout/EMT669/cycloids/cycloid.mov

■   Cycloid animation from Math Demos website: http://mathdemos.gcsu.edu/mathdemos/ cycloid-demo/

■   Graphing calculators

■   Spreadsheet to create a cycloid graph

■   Whiteboard, Smart Board, or chalkboard

CONTENT

Abby is riding her bike along the sidewalk and hears a clicking noise as the back wheel turns. Upon investigation (Figure 2.4), she discovers that her tire has a rock lodged in it that is hitting the ground each time the tire rotates. What would the path of the rock look like if it were graphed on the x–y axis, where x is the distance the bike goes and y is the height of the rock embedded in the wheel?

In Grades 9-12, students develop insights into mathematical abstraction and structure by exploring the behavior of nonlinear relationships for polynomial, exponential, rational, and periodic functions. When these relationships are embedded in various contexts such as Abby's bicycle problem, students are challenged to describe the motion using algebraic symbols to represent and explain the mathematical relationship. They develop tabular and graphical representations to aid in visualizing the mathematical situation. As they analyze the motion of the rock embedded in a bicycle wheel, they are engaged in the

FIGURE 2.4. There is a rock lodged in Abby's bike tire.

mathematical processes for identifying a specific functional notation for the motion. In this case two curves are explored: the sine curve and a cycloid curve.

PEDAGOGY

Introduce the problem with a video of a person riding a bike, such as the video *Bicycle Rock–Part 1*. Identify a location on the tire for the rock embedded in the wheel and focus the students' attention with two questions that arise from the video.

1. What is the relationship between the height of the rock off the ground and the distance that the tire travels as the person rides the bike?

2. What is the path of the rock as the person rides along?

Ask students to clarify the difference between the two questions. Encourage them to use the demonstration bike as they describe their interpretations. Challenge the students to consider how they might proceed in answering each of the questions. Use *Bicycle Rock– Part 2* or *Wheel with Graph* video from the Screening Room for discussing the questions.

The first question is concerned with the height of the rock in the tire from the ground versus the distance the tire travels. Select a particular point on the tire as if it were the rock. Ask students to sketch a graph of the height of the rock as a function of time as the tire rotates through one complete rotation. After sharing their ideas about the relationship, have students sketch their ideas of the graph of the height of the rock as a function of time. Create an animation of this process in Geometer's Sketchpad as depicted in

Figure 2.5A, B, and C. Hide the parallel line to the road line, the perpendicular line to the road line, and the center point of the circle for easier viewing of the animation as point A moves clockwise about the circle (as if the tire were rolling down the street).

Now have the students compare their data for their conjecture with the data displayed in the *Wheel with Numbers* video from the Screening Room. In this video, the height of the rock is measured from the line through the center of the tire and not the line representing the ground. Why are some of the values negative and some positive? What do the values from the video indicate about the measurement technique? How would your graph change if you used these data?

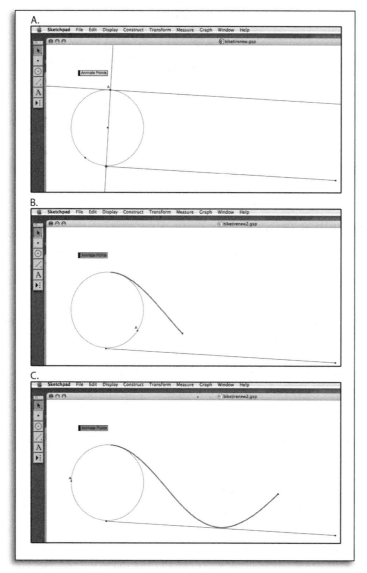

FIGURES 2.5A, B, C.
A Geometer's Sketchpad graphical animation sketching the graph of the height of the rock embedded in the tire (point A) as a function of the distance the tire travels.

After students have discussed and shared their graphs and ideas about the data from the video, show the *Wheel with Graph* video, which shows the tire movement and displays a graphical representation of the data generated. Ask students, "How is this graph similar to your graph?" Both graphs display the relationship of the height of the rock over time as a function of time. The difference between the video graph and the students' graphs comes from the line from which the rock height is measured. Figure 2.5 shows the measurements from the ground, while the *Wheel with Graph* video graphs the data measured from the diameter of the tire that is parallel to the ground. Both have the shape of a sine function.

The second question—What is the path of the rock as the person rides along?—is concerned with the path of the rock as the biker rides along the sidewalk. Have the students sketch their thinking about this question and propose a conjecture as to the graph for this question. Does the path of the rock describe the same function as the graph they determined for the question about the height of the rock as a function of time? After the students have posed a conjecture about the path, show them an animation of the path of the rock as a function of time (from the Jim Wilson website: http://jwilson.coe.uga.edu/EMT668/ EMT668.Student.Folders/BrombacherAarnout/EMT669/cycloids/cycloid.mov).

As animated in the video, Figure 2.6 describes a cycloid of the path of the rock as a function of time. A cycloid is a famous curve named by Galileo in 1599. It is the path traced out by a point on the circumference of a circle as the circle rolls (without slipping) along a straight line. Show the cycloid animation of the path of the rock on the circumference of the circular tire from the Math Demos website (http://mathdemos.gcsu.edu/mathdemos/ cycloid-demo/index.html).

The cycloid function is described as a parametric equation dependent on the radius, a, of the circle (the tire) where the ordered pairs of points are described as: $(x,y) = (a(t-\sin(t)), a(1-\cos(t)))$.

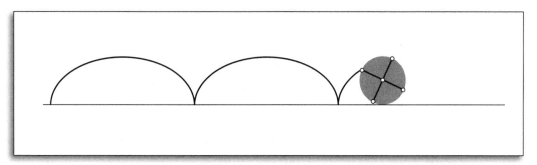

FIGURE 2.6. A graphical representation of the path of the rock on the tire as a function of time: a cycloid function.

TABLE 2.1. Data for the Path of the Rock on the Bike Tire as a Function of Time

TIME (IN SECONDS)	X	Y
0	0	0
1	1.902348182	5.51637233
2	13.08843088	16.99376204
3	34.3065599	23.87990996
4	57.08162994	19.84372345
5	71.5070913	8.596053774

Students can use their graphing calculators to identify a set of ordered pairs over the first 5 seconds of the rotation if the radius of the tire is 12 inches. Table 2.1 identifies the results over 5 seconds. Ask, "What is a graphical sketch of these points?"

Now, encourage the students to create a spreadsheet in which they enter the radius a of the tire and the time t is incremented by 0.2 seconds to generate the table of data. Plot enough data points to describe at least two revolutions of the tire. A spreadsheet with the formulas might look like the display in Figure 2.7. Note that the radius of the tire is in cell C5, where the formulas refer absolutely to this cell ($C$5).

Students should create a graph for x and y from the spreadsheet table, as in Figure 2.8, and explain the results. After they are comfortable with this description, explore the dynamic capability of this spreadsheet by changing the radius of the tire. What happens if the radius is 15 inches? If it is 20 inches? If it is 7 inches? The spreadsheet dynamically adjusts the table of data so the graph is immediately updated for newly calculated values.

MODIFICATIONS

Design a video of the changes in the spreadsheet as the radius of the tire is changed.
Challenge students to create a spreadsheet slider for the cell with the value for the radius (C5) in Figure 2.7. Ask students to use a movie screen capture software (such as Camtasia Studio for PCs or Snapz Pro X for Macs) to capture the changes in the graph as the slider is changed. As the value for the radius of the tire changes, the ordered pairs and the graphical description of the cycloid are dynamically changed to represent the new data.

◇	A	B	C
1			
2			
3	Graph of the path of the rock over time		
4			
5	Radius of the tire (inches):		12
6			
7	Time (in seconds)	x	y
8	0	=$C$5*(A8-SIN(A8))	=$C$5*(1-COS(A8))
9	=A8+0.2	=$C$5*(A9-SIN(A9))	=$C$5*(1-COS(A9))
10	=A9+0.2	=$C$5*(A10-SIN(A10))	=$C$5*(1-COS(A10))
11	=A10+0.2	=$C$5*(A11-SIN(A11))	=$C$5*(1-COS(A11))
12	=A11+0.2	=$C$5*(A12-SIN(A12))	=$C$5*(1-COS(A12))
13	=A12+0.2	=$C$5*(A13-SIN(A13))	=$C$5*(1-COS(A13))
14	=A13+0.2	=$C$5*(A14-SIN(A14))	=$C$5*(1-COS(A14))
15	=A14+0.2	=$C$5*(A15-SIN(A15))	=$C$5*(1-COS(A15))
16	=A15+0.2	=$C$5*(A16-SIN(A16))	=$C$5*(1-COS(A16))

FIGURE 2.7. Spreadsheet formulas to calculate the path of the rock over time.

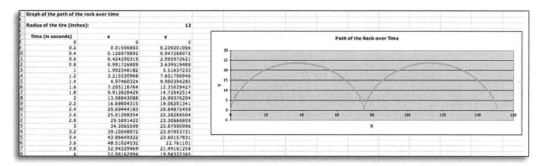

FIGURE 2.8. Spreadsheet table and graph of the path of the rock over time.

Vary the objects in motion. Consider similar projects for other objects in motion, such as a seesaw, a Ferris wheel, or another kind of carnival ride. Ask students, "What types of graphs are revealed?" Students can create videos of the motions, analyze the videos, and gather data for generating the graphs. Or they can simulate the motion of these different objects using Geometer's Sketchpad.

Consider different variables in the motion. Think about the force generated on a merry-go-round. What happens to the people on the ride as its speed is increased? Is there a difference if the person is sitting near the center versus the outer edge? Watch a video of the motion of children on a merry-go-round as it is moved at different speeds and as the children are sitting in different locations. Analyze the visual description by preparing a graph of the distance of the children's heads from the center as the merry-go-round moves at different speeds. Simulate the graph by entering data in a spreadsheet to create a graphical representation.

Rates of Change
Mathematics–Rate
GRADE LEVELS: 7–10

Objective

■ The speed of a car is identified as the number of miles traveled in an hour. In this activity, students will investigate how police aircraft are able to determine the speed of cars from the air.

National Council of Teachers of Mathematics (NCTM) Standards Addressed

■ Represent and analyze mathematical situations and structures using algebraic symbols (NCTM, Algebra Standard Grades 6–8, 9–12)

■ Analyze change in various contexts—use graphical and symbolic representations (NCTM, Algebra Standard Grades 6–8, 9–12)

■ Use visualization, spatial reasoning, and geometric modeling to solve problems (NCTM, Geometry Standard Grades 6–8, 9–12)

National Educational Technology Standards for Students (NETS·S) Addressed

1. **Creativity and Innovation**

    a. apply existing knowledge to generate new ideas, products, or processes

    c. use models and simulations to explore complex systems and issues

3. **Research and Information Fluency**

    a. plan strategies to guide inquiry

    d. process data and report results

4. **Critical Thinking, Problem Solving, and Decision Making**

    a. identify and define authentic problems and significant questions for investigation

    c. collect and analyze data to identify solutions and make informed decisions

6. **Technology Operations and Concepts**

    a. understand and use technology systems

Technology/Materials Needed

■ Aviation video found in the Aviation section of the Ohio State Patrol website: http://statepatrol. ohio.gov/units.stm#Aviation. (Click on "Aviation Video.") The relevant part of the video runs from 1 minute 40 seconds to 4 minutes 35 seconds. You can also save this video to your computer and watch it offline (or edit out the unnecessary sections and keep it for future use—see Chapter 6: "Acquiring Digital Video").

CONTENT

Rate is an important concept in mathematics. It is introduced in pre-algebra under the auspices of slope. Many students do not make the connection between rates of change and slope. A rate can be defined as a distance traveled divided by a time interval. For the rate of a car in motion, consider the ratio of the distance traveled to the amount of time to drive that distance. Most cars do not travel at a constant speed, so rate is usually defined as an average rate or speed.

PEDAGOGY

Display an image of a highway speed limit sign along with an image of a sign that says "Speed Limit Enforced by Aircraft" (Figure 2.9). Ask students, "What do these signs actually mean? How can an aircraft know how fast you are going and, furthermore, stop you to give you a ticket?"

Aircraft enforcement is traffic enforcement used in open spaces and on the interstate systems. Although it does not produce exact results, this manner of determining the speed of vehicles is accepted in a court of law. Tell students that they are going to determine how this process works.

FIGURE 2.9. Example of highway sign for rates-of-change activity.

Show students the relevant portion of the aviation video and discuss the simple idea used by police officers in Ohio. The police in the aircraft have a stopwatch to determine the amount of time a car takes to travel from one point to another. The points are predetermined, chosen for clear views from the aircraft and a safe place for a ground vehicle to stop the car. Next time you notice the sign on the highway, look down at the road under the sign. You will often see a line painted perpendicular to the traffic flow. Another line is painted some distance away. These lines signal the predetermined points. Once the points have been determined, a trial run is made to assure accuracy of the distance and time.

Now the police are ready to catch a speeder from the aircraft. A police car on the ground gets into position in preparation for stopping the offender quickly. The policeman in the aircraft starts a stopwatch when a car crosses the first line and stops the watch when it crosses the second line. This information is used to determine the speed of the car. If the car is speeding, the officer in the aircraft radios the make, color, and speed of the car to the officer in the police car, who then stops and cites the violator.

The question for students is, "How do the police officers determine a car's speed based on the information gathered from the aircraft?" Show students the video of police aircraft timing a car several times (from the Ohio State Patrol website).

Tell students that the simplest way to determine the rate of the car is to use a stopwatch to record the amount of time it takes for the car to travel the distance from the starting point to the stopping point. The following questions can be used to engage students in discourse about their analysis of the vehicle's speed:

- What is the average rate of speed of the car?

- What are the units for this rate?

- Do you think that the car has the same rate in this video as at other times?

- Why is it important that the police monitor travelers in this manner?

MODIFICATIONS

Vary the view of the moving object. Calculate the average rate of speed of a runner in a video as the runner progresses across a large screen display at the front of the room. Have students mark starting and stopping points they plan to use from the video display of the runner. Have multiple groups gather data to demonstrate a variance in the rates. Use these different rates to calculate an average rate of speed for the runner. Vary this activity by having groups videotape various objects in motion (such as a car, tractor, train, or bus). Students might also watch or make their own video of objects of different sizes and weights falling from some height, then calculate the average rate of speed of the falling objects, comparing their speeds.

Capture videos of students at a track meet. Have students analyze the process to be used for designing videos of student races at a track meet, such as of a runner in a race. Students are to determine various kinds of markers that could be used for their measurements in the video. Have students analyze the speed of the runner from their observations of the videos made by others. Students can also videotape a person walking from one point to another point. Again, they should discover the data needed to determine the average rate at which a person is walking.

Creating Digital Video Activity

EVEN WHEN students create their own video, they can also engage in watching and analyzing. In fact, many of the modifications in the previous activities have presented ideas for students creating mathematics videos.

A large majority of students beyond third grade have probably viewed YouTube clips. They enjoy the clips and even send them to their family, friends, and teachers via e-mail. Check out the YouTube video clip called *What Do You Know about Math?* (www.youtube. com/watch?v=Ooa8nHKPZ5k). Some students and teachers are even creating their own videos to post on YouTube. See how one teacher's video displays a parallel-line dance in a YouTube video called *Crazy Math Teacher: The Dance of the Parallel Lines* (www.youtube. com/watch?v=mVb6wpNRz9c). Such videos are easy to create. Students can use their cell phones to capture the video while the teacher dances to the music.

Creating videos can be as simple as taking pictures and creating slide shows, adding audio and transition effects. Some students have access to cameras that can record movies. Note how an elementary school student, Madeline, describes the mathematics she knows and how she thinks about it in a YouTube video called *Math With Madeline* (www.youtube.com/watch?v=EyHER6o-4xo). Or view the YouTube video *Finite Simple Group (of Order Two)* (www.youtube.com/watch?v=BipvGD-LCjU), in which college students sing about their understanding of some abstract mathematical ideas.

Using digital video equipment to learn mathematics is not a traditional strategy in mathematics classrooms. However, given that students are actively making videos outside of school, you should consider allowing students to use this medium for communicating what they know and are able to complete. With the proliferation of video technologies and the decreased cost of purchasing digital equipment, students in elementary through high school are likely to have access to digital video equipment.

Students can create several types of videos to enhance learning in the mathematics classroom. They might use digital video equipment to create a teaching video in which they teach a mathematical concept or process. For example, they might develop a script and create a video to instruct how to compute $(2x + 3)^2$. Maybe they can use a computer

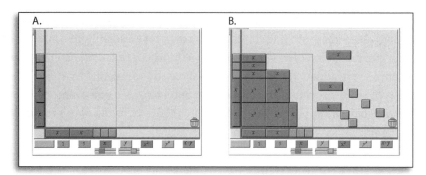

FIGURES 2.10A and B. Multiplying algebraic expressions with virtual manipulatives.

screen capture to show how to use Algebra Tiles (Figures 2.10A and B from the online National Library of Virtual Manipulatives) to demonstrate that the product of $(2x + 3)$ $(2x + 3)$—Figure 2.10A—creates a rectangle that must be covered by blocks that represent $4x^2 + 12x + 9$—Figure 2.10B.

Students might create a "how-to" video to explain a particular mathematical process, such as multiplication of fractions. Students might also create a video showing how to use the classroom calculators to enter data, graph a scatter plot, find the regression equation, and graph the regression equation on the scatter plot.

What about assessing students' knowledge by having them create videos? Imagine how you might assess student understanding in a society where digital video capabilities extend communication possibilities in the classroom. Instruct small groups of two or three students to create a video that shows each student completing problems in which they explain what they learned in class that day. Have students in each group pick one problem from the homework set and show how to complete that problem in the video. The problems shown by the groups should present differing aspects of the content. For example, when the students are introduced to the method for factoring the difference of two perfect squares during the classroom instruction, one student might show how to factor $a^2 - 64$, another student $9x^2 - 100y^6$, and a third student $3x^8 - 3$. Thus, the various problems increase in difficulty. (Encourage students to create a script before they begin capturing video.)

Research shows that the best way to learn is to teach or communicate the idea to others. Students might create a video that teaches another person (their siblings, parents, other students, other teachers) specific mathematical concepts or ideas, such as variables or the ways geometry is used in local buildings. The number of school-aged students submitting videos to YouTube indicates that they clearly enjoy this creative outlet.

Train Switcheroo
Mathematics–Problem Solving
GRADE LEVELS: 3–9

Objectives

- Students solve problems that arise in contexts outside of mathematics.

- Students organize and consolidate their mathematical thinking through communication.

- Students create and use visual representations to organize, record, and communicate their solutions to problems.

National Council of Teachers of Mathematics (NCTM) Standards Addressed

- Build new mathematical knowledge through problem solving (NCTM, Problem Solving Standard Grades PK–12)

- Select and use various types of reasoning and methods of proof (NCTM, Reasoning and Proof Standard Grades PK–12)

- Communicate their mathematical thinking coherently and clearly to peers, teachers, and others (NCTM, Communication Standard Grades PK–12)

- Recognize and apply mathematics in contexts outside of mathematics (NCTM, Connections Standard Grades PK–12)

- Use representations to model and interpret physical, social, and mathematical phenomena (NCTM, Representation Standard Grades PK–12)

National Educational Technology Standards for Students (NETS·S) Addressed

1. **Creativity and Innovation**

   a. apply existing knowledge to generate new ideas, products, or processes

   c. use models and simulations to explore complex systems and issues

2. **Communication and Collaboration**

   a. interact, collaborate, and publish with peers, experts, or others employing a variety of digital environments and media

   b. communicate information and ideas effectively to multiple audiences using a variety of media and formats

3. **Research and Information Fluency**

   a. plan strategies to guide inquiry

4. **Critical Thinking, Problem Solving, and Decision Making**

   a. identify and define authentic problems and significant questions for investigation

   b. plan and manage activities to develop a solution or complete a project

   d. use multiple processes and diverse perspectives to explore alternative solutions

6. **Technology Operations and Concepts**

   a.   understand and use technology systems

Technology/Materials Needed

- Cell phone, digital cameras with movie settings, or inexpensive camcorders for video capture

- Sample student video solution on YouTube: "Math problem" (www.youtube.com/watch?v=Jy2hS0fOOsg&feature=e-mail)

- Toy engine and train cars to model problem

CONTENT

Mathematics is famous for problems that deal with trains. Do you recall problems like the following?

If two trains leave the station at the same time, one traveling east and the other traveling west, how long will it take them to be 330 miles apart if the eastbound train is traveling at an average of 60 miles per hour and the westbound train is traveling at an average of 50 miles per hour?

The solution to this problem is typically found with an equation. This activity considers a problem not so easily solved by an equation—the "train switcheroo" problem posed by the EQUALS program at the Lawrence Hall of Science, University of California at Berkeley, in 1982.

Problem solving is an integral part of mathematics because it helps students build new mathematical knowledge. When engaged in problem solving, students develop "ways of thinking, habits of persistence and curiosity, and confidence in unfamiliar situations that will serve them well outside the mathematics classroom" (NCTM, 2000, p. 52). An important part of the problem-solving process is communicating how a problem can be solved. As students share their methods, they develop more mathematical ways of communicating. Creating digital videos of problem solutions provides a fun visual medium for mathematical communication.

PEDAGOGY

Figure 2.11 displays the basic framework for the problem: the tracks, two cars, and the engine. The engine is currently on the right offshoot of the circular track. Cars A and B are on opposites sides of the track. There is a tunnel on the track, but only the train can go through the tunnel. The train can push and pull the cars. Note that turns are not possible at each of the offshoot corners. The task is to switch the cars and return the engine to its starting position.

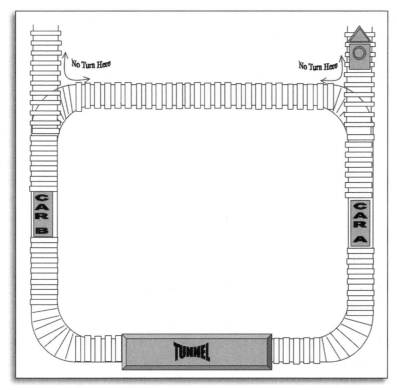

FIGURE 2.11. The train track and starting positions for the cars and the engine in the Train Switcheroo problem.

In addition to the technology, you will need a toy engine and train cars to model the problem and the solution on a classroom-created railroad track. On Day 1 of this one-week activity, introduce the problem using the toy engine, cars, and a railroad track. Model the legal actions: the engine can push and pull, only the engine can go through the tunnel, and no turns can be made at the offshoots. Make sure students understand the problem and the challenges.

Students have 1 week to identify a solution and prepare a presentation that explains their set of instructions for switching Car A and Car B and returning the engine to its starting place in the same orientation. Suggest that they think of creative ways of communicating their solutions, such as creating a digital video to help the class visualize the steps in the solutions. The video might be of their family acting out the solution, where Mom is Car A, Dad is Car B, and the student is the engine. A sample student video on YouTube (www.youtube.com/watch?v=Jy2hSofOOsg&feature=e-mail) shows Justin directing his mom (engine), his younger brother Joel (Car B), and his sister Jodi (Car A) to demonstrate a possible solution to the problem, using their living room for the train track and his dad as the videographer. Alternatively, students might video a model that uses their own railroad track, toy cars, and engine as a demonstration for the class.

Check daily on students' progress. You can even show a solution on the overhead using toy models to show them that the problem can be completed. Some teachers have found that even when students are shown a solution, they do not catch all the steps and have to rethink the solution and how to communicate it. Besides, the problem has many possible solutions. Ask students if they can find a more efficient solution than the one you demonstrated.

On the due date, students should present their videos or other ways of expressing the solution (e.g., a play they perform, a bulletin board that shows the progression of the steps, or even a list of steps to the solution). Discuss the differences in the communications of the solutions and how some are more visual than others. Ask them why a visual approach is useful in imagining the solution.

MODIFICATIONS

Vary the problem. Pose the famous locker problem that begins at a school that has 100 lockers, all shut. Suppose the first student goes along the row and opens every locker. The second student then goes along and shuts every other locker beginning with locker No. 2. The third student changes the state of every third locker beginning with locker No. 3. (If the locker is open, the student shuts it; if the locker is closed, the student opens it.) The fourth student changes the state of every fourth locker beginning with No. 4. Imagine that this process continues until 100 students have followed the pattern with the 100 lockers. At the end, which lockers are open and which are closed? Which lockers have been switched most often? How many lockers, and which ones, were touched exactly five times? Create a video that models the solution for a subset of the 100 lockers (say, 20 lockers).

Introduce a problem with a digital video. Ask students to pose a problem for the class to solve using a video presentation of a problem. They might create a mathematical mystery. They might construct an object and challenge students to find the volume of the object. Or they might tackle the mystery of the Towers of Hanoi. Such modifications put the students in the position of identifying a problem that requires more analysis than typical workbook problems.

Marching Band Choreography
Mathematics–Geometry
GRADE LEVELS: 6–12

Objectives

- Students analyze movements graphically and algebraically.

- Students use transformations and symmetry to create a choreographed piece.

- Students make connections between a real-world model and a mathematical model.

- Students use mathematical language to describe their model.

National Council of Teachers of Mathematics (NCTM) Standards Addressed

- Use mathematical models to represent and understand quantitative relationships—model and solve relations and functions through graphical representations (NCTM, Algebra Standard Grades 6–8, 9–12)

- Analyze change in various contexts—use graphical and symbolic representations (NCTM, Algebra Standard Grades 6–8, 9–12)

- Apply transformations and use symmetry to analyze mathematical situations (NCTM, Geometry Standard Grades 6–8, 9–12)

- Use visualization, spatial reasoning, and geometric modeling to solve problems (NCTM, Geometry Standard Grades 6–8, 9–12)

- Use the language of mathematics to express mathematical ideas precisely (NCTM, Communication Standard Grades PK–12)

National Educational Technology Standards for Students (NETS·S) Addressed

1. **Creativity and Innovation**

    a. apply existing knowledge to generate new ideas, products, or processes

    b. create original works as a means of personal or group expression

    c. use models and simulations to explore complex systems and issues

2. **Communication and Collaboration**

    a. interact, collaborate, and publish with peers, experts, or others employing a variety of digital environments and media

    d. contribute to project teams to produce original works or solve problems

3. **Research and Information Fluency**

    c. evaluate and select information sources and digital tools based on the appropriateness to specific tasks

4. **Critical Thinking, Problem Solving, and Decision Making**

    a. identify and define authentic problems and significant questions for investigation

    b. plan and manage activities to develop a solution or complete a project

    c. collect and analyze data to identify solutions and make informed decisions

6. **Technology Operations and Concepts**

    a. understand and use technology systems

    b. select and use applications effectively and productively

Technology/Materials Needed

- IUP Marching Band clip: www.youtube.com/watch?v=1ufaXxcm0ao
- Digital video camera
- Graphing calculator such as the TI-83 Plus
- TI Interactive! (optional)
- Smart Board, whiteboard, or chalkboard

CONTENT

Dance, gymnastics, skating, baton twirling, and cheerleading routines all have a designed set of movements. This set of movements is choreography, which literally means "dance-writing" and is also known as "dance composition." It is the art of making movement structures by connecting them.

One of the most complicated forms of choreography is that used by a band director for a marching band and its formations. A marching band not only performs musical compositions but also entertains with steps and movements to create designs such as letters, logos, or even animated pictures. The members must mark time, change directions, change styles of stepping, and march forward and backward, all while playing the designated music with their instruments. Band directors must create sets of movements for their band members that are coordinated with the music and visually appealing to an audience watching from both the ground level and the stands above. Certain instruments must be kept together to provide the best sound for the music. The drill team, twirlers, and flag team members must also coordinate their movements with the band's.

To choreograph all of this, band directors must document the movements of each person on the field. Figures 2.12A, B, and C document specific formations designed by David Martynuik, marching band director at Indiana University of Pennsylvania (IUP).

Geometry is more than definitions, theorems, and proofs. Geometry involves analyzing shapes and structures and their relationships. Transformations such as transltions, rotations, and reflections are important geometrical ideas. Identifying centers of rotations, lines of reflection, and positions of pre-images and images are key to the identification of and communication about symmetry. Rotational symmetry and lines of symmetry

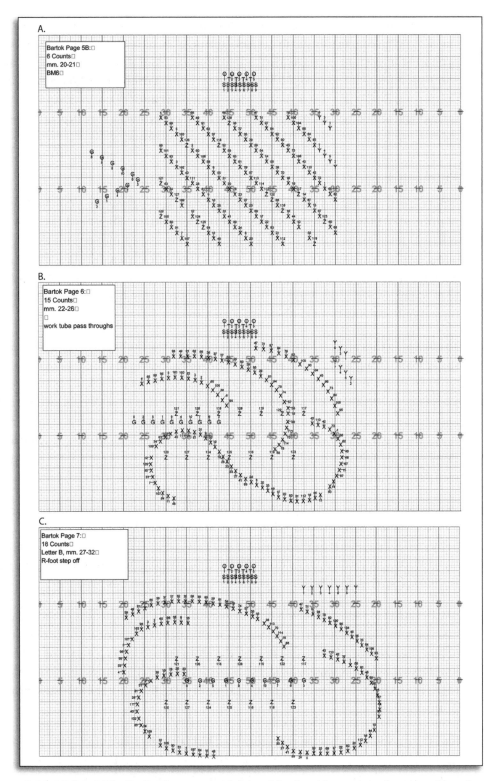

FIGURES 2.12A, B, C. Three sequential marching band formations choreographing the band's movements.

are used in determining congruence or dilations, such as magnifications and contractions. Making connections among these geometrical ideas with algebraic representations is another important mathematical way of knowing and thinking. Communicating symbolic representations for multiple parallel lines is useful in modeling and interpreting physical phenomena such as those found in band formations. Analyzing band formations provides students with visualization experiences that support the development of algebraic and geometrical thinking and reasoning.

PEDAGOGY

Before creating a digital video of a choreographed piece, students first must be guided to think about the mathematics of the various formations. They need to watch videos of different formations and identify potential mathematical functions for the formations being displayed. They need experiences in mathematically analyzing the actions in which they defend their analyses for the mathematics involved in the formation. These preparatory experiences are essential before students can begin creating their own formations evolving from mathematical functions.

To engage in this process, you might begin by showing the three-minute YouTube clip of the IUP Marching Band to the students to introduce them to the challenge of analyzing the marching band formations. Ask students to watch the video and identify concepts of mathematics in the band's movements as they watch the video. Encourage them to think about timing, counting, symmetry, shapes, transformations, and other patterns. After they have watched the video, have the students share their ideas. You might use questions such as, "What geometrical ideas are used in creating these formations that are visually appealing? What algebraic ideas are used?"

Reshow the clip. The best way to begin the analysis of the band formations is to project the scene onto a Smart Board, whiteboard, or chalkboard so that you can stop it at key points to show symmetry, translations, and polygons. Use the Smart Board pen, dry-erase marker, or chalk to draw the shape or figure that has been created in the video. Encourage students to identify their observations in this same way.

The first part of the clip shows a neat formation where the members of the band are marching in diagonal lines. Stop the clip at 28 seconds and have students create a graph of how the band members are standing. Either the graphing calculator or TI Interactive! provides an excellent tool for students to explore the various lines that are formed. Figure 2.13 shows one possible configuration created by using the software program TI Interactive!

Figure 2.14 shows this same configuration, but with the coordinate axes added. In this figure, the student placed the y-axis on the 35-yard line, but the band director needs the y-axis on the 50-yard line. Challenge students to create this formation so that the y-axis is on the 50-yard line to split the center group of band members and form a more pleasing formation. This exploration is useful in aiding students in understanding linear

FIGURE 2.13. Band configuration displayed using TI Interactive!

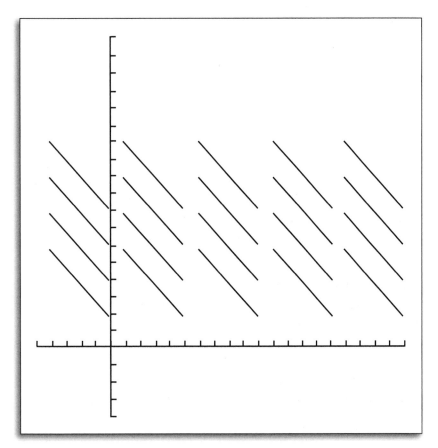

FIGURE 2.14. Addition of the coordinate axes to the band configuration.

functions. Even though the slopes are all the same for these lines, students develop a comprehensive understanding of intercepts and domains.

Many other formations from the YouTube clip display a symmetric choreography. For example, stop the video clip at 2:02 minutes. The band is completely symmetrical on both sides of the 50-yard line. Furthermore, there are vertical lines, inverse absolute value relations, and even part of an elliptical function. This formation can also be modeled with equations on a graphing calculator. Figures 2.15A and B show this formation using a TI-83 Plus graphing calculator, as well as the window used to create the formation. The y-axis represents the 50-yard line and the x-axis is in the middle of the field, such that the intersection of the x–y axis is at the center of the field. The equations used for this formation are:

$$Y_1 = (20)(X > -15)(X < 15)$$

$$Y_2 = (X-10)(X > 10)(X < 30)$$

$$Y_3 = (-X + 10)(X > 10)(X < 30)$$

$$Y_4 = (-X-10)(X > -30)(X < -10)$$

$$Y_5 = (X + 10)(X > -30)(X < -10)$$

$$Y_6 = (-5X + 50)(X > 10)(X < 14)$$

$$Y_7 = (5X + 50)(X > -14)(X < -10)$$

$$Y_8 = -(SQRT(400 -X^2)/2) + 20$$

After the discussion of the clip is completed, challenge students in groups of five or six to create a symmetrical formation or one that uses one of the other mathematical concepts that have been discussed. After the groups pose for a digital photo, the rest of the class is expected to determine what mathematical concepts are being depicted in the photos.

As a weeklong project, students in small groups should map out a set of movements for their group that includes several of the mathematical concepts discussed. One group might be assigned to map out a set of movements using transformations, another group using shapes, and still another group using symmetry. More advanced students should be challenged to design a combination of movements based on a set of functions, such as linear, quadratic, cubic, piecewise, periodic, or exponential. Domain or asymptotic constraints could also be given to students. Allow students to use a graphing calculator or any other technology that might help them to design the movements.

After students have mapped out their movements on paper and have designed the sequence of steps, have them practice several times before someone videos them doing the choreographed piece. When students describe their proposed creations, they need to

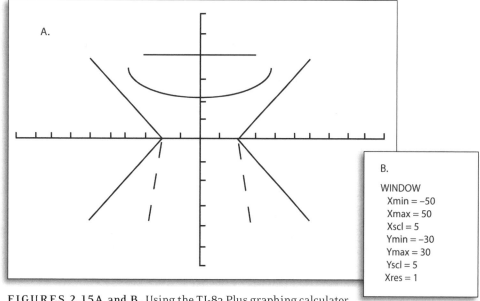

FIGURES 2.15A and B. Using the TI-83 Plus graphing calculator to display the band formation.

describe the mathematical functions that led to the creation. Challenge the students also to set their movements to music. Videotaping the movements calls for careful consideration. In order to see the mathematical functions, the videos likely need to be captured on a football field or in a basketball court, where the person with the camera can be stationed above ground level as the movements are performed. The music might even be dubbed using a program such as iMovie for the Mac or Movie Maker for the PC.

As students complete their video, they should share them with the rest of the class, asking class members to analyze mathematically the motions used in the choreographed formation. Such video productions provide an outlet for students' artistic talents while also communicating mathematics. Equally important, focusing on the mathematical functions of the formations helps students extend the abstractions of mathematics to the world around them.

MODIFICATIONS

Specify particular types of formations. Challenge groups of three or four students to create dances that incorporate only symmetry or only transformations. After creating videos of their dances, they should challenge the members of the class to identify the specific mathematics in the videos.

Specify particular functions to be expressed. Create some videos of a student walking in front of a camera in the movement of a given function. For example, if the teacher asks the student to move in front of the camera in the shape of the function $y = abs(x)$, the student should start about 3 meters away from the camera, walk toward the camera at a constant rate, and then walk away from the camera at the same constant rate. A student can be taped moving in front of the camera, and other students can try to figure out the path of that person, either by graphing the movement or by defining it as a function. Higher level students should be encouraged to express movements as piecewise functions.

Conclusion

"TECHNOLOGY IS essential in teaching and learning mathematics; it influences the mathematics that is taught and enhances students' learning" (NCTM, 2000, p. 24). Digital videos are technologies with the capabilities for enhancing students' learning of mathematics. Digital videos have the potential for engaging students in mathematical thinking. Creative teachers challenge traditional ways of learning mathematics in which students spend hours and hours with paper and pencil, practicing processes that lead to solutions of bland problems.

When adding digital videos to the pedagogical mix, teachers can challenge students to reflect on what is said and done in ways that ultimately engage them in important mathematical processes: reasoning and problem solving. Adding digital videos to the classroom recognizes one of the ways that students are engaged in communicating what they know and understand. Communicating about mathematics is an essential ingredient for clarifying their reasoning and understanding. Creating videos provides ways to meet this goal. Integrating digital videos with additional dynamic media such as Geometer's Sketchpad, spreadsheets, calculators, and virtual manipulatives affords students with opportunities to create, use, and make sense of multiple representations of mathematical ideas.

Analysis of activities with digital videos can be accomplished along with these dynamic technologies to support students' reasoning and thinking as they work to understand mathematical concepts and processes. Mathematics is far more than the content areas of numbers, algebra, geometry, probability and statistics, and measurement. NCTM's process standards—problem solving, reasoning and proof, communication, connections, and representation—highlight the ways of acquiring and using knowledge in the multiple mathematical content areas.

Digital videos are tools that effective mathematics teachers can incorporate into their pedagogical toolkits. This chapter provides an initial look at how videos might be integrated with the activities students are engaged in to learn mathematics, where videos are watched, analyzed, and created. Keep in mind the challenges of using videos in mathematics classrooms. The mathematics curriculum is extensive. However, the capabilities of digital videos are connected with students' ways of knowing, learning, and doing as they develop their mathematical thinking at a deeper level.

References

Analysis. (2010). In *Merriam-Webster's online dictionary*. Retrieved January 20, 2010, from www.merriam-webster.com/dictionary/analysis

Garofalo, J. (2006, January). *Which technologies to incorporate into teacher preparation, including goals, rationales and relative emphases?* Workshop presented at the annual meeting of the Association of Mathematics Teacher Educators, Tampa, FL.

International Society for Technology in Education. (2007). *National educational technology standards for students* (2nd ed.). Eugene, OR: Author.

Keller, J. M. (1987). Development and use of the ARCS model of instructional design. *Journal of Instructional Development*, *10*(3), 2-10.

National Council of Teachers of Mathematics. (2000). *Principles and standards for school mathematics*. Reston, VA: Author.

CHAPTER 3

John C. Park

digital video in science education

SCIENCE IS frequently a visual endeavor, dependent on observations made directly or indirectly. In the science classroom, teachers have long employed motion pictures to allow students to make indirect observations when needed to animate events, show hazardous experiments, and view special effects such as time-lapse and slow-motion photography or extreme close-ups and microphotography.

New technology has multiplied the ways in which digital video can enhance science learning:

■ Video demonstrations can replace live demonstrations that may not always work or that involve potential hazard.

■ Video demonstrations allow students to review content after an absence or if they need additional work.

■ Stop-motion animations can assist students in understanding scientific processes or mechanisms.

■ Proper laboratory skills can be demonstrated via video to help students learn how to operate scientific equipment.

■ Interactive object movies can provide a three-dimensional aspect to inspecting models and specimens.

■ Interactive panoramas can enable a three-dimensional view of a location for visual inspection.

■ Motion and time measurements can be made of video-recorded events.

■ Video of a specific event can be synchronized with related data.

■ Students can take measurements and make inferences from popular Hollywood movies to see if the scenes are probable or even possible.

■ Video can be embedded for observation in assessment instruments such as multiple-choice tests.

■ Desktop demonstrations can be enlarged for full classroom viewing using a projector.

Digital Video and Pedagogy of Science Inquiry

FROM THE early days of school science in the United States to the modern classroom today, the learning of science has focused on student inquiry. Robert Karplus proposed a pedagogical strategy for teaching science called the "learning cycle" (Fuller, 2002). The original pedagogy of exploration, invention, and discovery has been implemented, researched, and revised over the last four decades. Research supports the claim that the correct use of the learning cycle in the science classroom at all levels is effective in helping students move toward stated objectives of science understanding.

TABLE 3.1. Examples of Video Use in the Five-E Instructional Model

STAGE	VIDEO EXAMPLE
ENGAGE	Students watch a video of a kernel of popcorn popping in slow motion. During the engage stage, this video generates interest, because most students have not seen the event in slow motion, and raises the question of what causes popcorn kernels to burst. Find the video at www.youtube.com/watch?v=CXDstfD9eJ0.
EXPLORE	Students examine a video of a sealed drum of hot water vapor that is cooled in an ice bath and then collapses. During the exploration stage, the students test their predictions and hypotheses, generate new predictions, try alternative ideas, and record their observations and ideas. Students videotape their own versions of the event using soda cans or other sealable thin-walled metal cans and generate explanations for why the can behaves as it does. Find the initial video at www.youtube.com/watch?v=j2k40Hw3Gl0.
EXPLAIN	Students investigate a video that shows flames of four candles of various heights in an aquarium being extinguished by an unseen method, the shortest candle being extinguished first and the tallest last. Students explain possible solutions or answers to others, listen critically to others' explanations, and defend explanations using evidence from the video. Students create a video that illustrates their explanation. Find the "Candles" video at http://site.aace.org/video/books/teaching/science.
ELABORATE	Students have just completed activities that assist in their understanding of the phases of the moon. In the elaboration stage, students apply new terms, use explanations and skills in a new but similar situation, draw conclusions from evidence, record observations and explanations, and check one another for understanding. Students view the video animation of phases of the Earth as viewed from the moon. They answer questions regarding phases of the moon as seen from the Earth at given points in the video (for example, if the Earth's phase is full as observed from the moon, what phase is the moon in as observed from the Earth?). The video can be found at www.ncsu.edu/sciencejunction/PhaseEarth.mov.
EVALUATE	Students demonstrate an understanding or knowledge of a concept or skill. For example, a student creates a video on how to properly measure the mass of a nickel to the nearest 0.1 gram using a triple beam balance.

The latest revision that is widely accepted in the science education community is the Biological Sciences Curriculum Studies (BSCS) "Five-E" instructional model (Bybee, Powell, & Trowbridge, 2008). This model consists of five stages: engage, explore, explain, elaborate, and evaluate. Digital video can provide the prompt for discussion in each of the stages of the learning cycle. Table 3.1 provides examples of ways digital video can be used in each stage at various grade levels.

Students should develop science process skills as they investigate science through inquiry. For upper elementary school students, basic skills include observing, inferring, measuring, communicating, classifying, and predicting. Middle and high school students should develop integrated science process skills, including controlling variables, defining operationally, formulating hypotheses, interpreting data, experimenting, and formulating models.

The activities presented in this chapter are divided into three categories that identify the primary activity in which students are engaged: watching digital video, analyzing digital video, and creating digital video. Watching videos that display science concepts allows students to use specific science process skills, including observing, inferring, classifying, and predicting. The analysis of videos enables students to practice the science process skills of measuring, communicating, and generating hypotheses. The creation of video allows others to explore science by interpreting data, experimenting, and formulating models. The creation of video also allows students to communicate the science they have learned to a broad audience.

Watching Digital Video Activities

WATCHING DIGITAL video can capture students' attention and engage them in the topic being introduced. If the digital video is carefully crafted, it can also be used to help students explore concepts and gain understanding through explanations within the video. Viewers can compare what happens as variables are changed in sequenced scenes, or they may be challenged by questions in overlaid titles or voice-overs. Other videos can be used to elaborate or to apply concepts discussed in class to new situations. For example, after doing activities related to average velocity, a video could be viewed that shows the velocity of a car traveling at 55 mph as viewed from a car next to it traveling at the same velocity. A sequence of these types of shots would introduce the students to the concepts of relative velocity and frame of reference.

Watching digital video can also be used to evaluate student understanding of concepts. For instance, you could generate a video quiz item on which students must identify the forces acting on a bubble rising though a tube of water shown in the video. Therefore, the watching of digital video can facilitate each of the stages of the Five-E learning cycle. The following two activities illustrate activities in which students can learn by watching downloadable media.

> **CONTENT STANDARDS**
>
> The National Science Education Standards are sponsored by the National Research Council and published by the National Academies Press, www.nap.edu/readingroom/books/nses/.

Exploring the Speed of Sound
Physics–Sound
GRADE LEVELS: 5–8

Objective

- Students discover that the detection of sound is not instantaneous to the event; it takes time for sound waves to travel through the air from the event to the observer.

National Science Education Standards (National Research Council, 1996) Addressed

All Levels Content Standard A:

- Abilities necessary to do scientific inquiry

Levels 5–8 Content Standard B:

- Develop an understanding of the transfer of energy

National Educational Technology Standards for Students (NETS·S) Addressed

1. **Creativity and Innovation**
   c. use models and simulations to explore complex systems and issues
   d. identify trends and forecast possibilities

4. **Critical Thinking, Problem Solving, and Decision Making**
   c. collect and analyze data to identify solutions and make informed decisions

Technology/Materials Needed

- *Speed of Sound I* video—found on the SITE Screening Room at http://site.aace.org/video/books/teaching/science
- *Speed of Sound II* video—found at http://site.aace.org/video/books/teaching/science
- At least one computer
- Projector and set of speakers if you will be projecting the video for the entire class
- Headphones, if the students are viewing the video on separate computers, so they can clearly identify the sounds for time comparison

CONTENT

The topic of wave characteristics is found in most state science curricula. Sound waves are of particular interest because students have familiar experiences with sound in everyday life. Students are expected to know about frequency (pitch), amplitude (loudness), and the speed at which sound travels through matter. In this particular case, students will notice the time difference between seeing an event occur and hearing the sound generated from that event. The students should be able to determine that the speed of light (what they see in the video) is greater than the speed of sound (what they hear in the video).

TECHNOLOGY

Two videos should be accessed before beginning the activity, *Speed of Sound I* and *Speed of Sound II.* Downloading the video to each computer hard drive will minimize any time lag or pauses that are typical when viewing the video over the Internet.

You will need at least one computer and, if you project the video for the entire class, a projector and set of speakers so the entire class can hear it clearly. If the students are viewing the video on separate computers, they should use headphones so they can clearly identify the sounds for time comparison.

PEDAGOGY

Engage

Students should watch *Speed of Sound I*, which shows a student, Preston, clapping two aluminum pots together at distances from 30 meters to 240 meters at 30-meter intervals (Figure 3.1). The movie can be displayed either as a demonstration controlled

FIGURE 3.1. Images from *Speed of Sound I.*

FIGURE 3.2. Images showing the addition of the two-way radio in *Speed of Sound II*.

by the teacher or by students using their own computer. Students should answer the following question while watching the movie: "What do you notice about the relationship between the distance of the event from the camera and the sound you hear?"

Direct students to note when they see the aluminum pots hit each other and when they hear the sound. As students view the video, they might not notice much at the 30-, 60-, and 90-meter marks. As the distance gets progressively longer, however, they should notice a delay between the clapping and the sound as detected by the camera: the longer the distance, the longer the delay in the sound. Ask students, "Why does apparent sound lag occur? Why is the lag not noticed at the shorter distances?"

Explore

To more clearly demonstrate this time lag between when the event occurs and when the sound is heard, students should view a second digital movie, *Speed of Sound II*, of the same event. Explain to students before they view the video what they will be seeing so they can focus on the appropriate data. This time, another student, Kelsey, joins Preston with a two-way radio. Kelsey will press the key on the radio while Preston claps the aluminum pots. A second radio was held beside the camera while taping. Two sounds can be heard on the video: the sound transmitted by the two-way radio, and the sound propagated through the air from the pots to the camera. See Figure 3.2 for images from this digital video.

As students watch the video, they will notice that two distinct noises can be distinguished with each clap of the aluminum pots. One is the sound transmitted by the radio, and one is the sound transmitted through the air from the pots to the camera. Ask students, "Which sound do you hear first? Why? What does the time difference between the two sounds represent?"

The sound they heard first is the sound transmitted through the two-way radio. The two-way radio transmits via radio waves that travel at the speed of light. Therefore, the time at which the sound was transmitted by the radio is a close representation of the time when the sound was generated. Therefore, the time difference between the two sounds represents the time it took for the sound to be propagated through the air to the camera. Ask the students about other instances where there is a time lag between seeing an event and hearing the sound (examples include the crack of the bat at a professional baseball park and the bang of exploding fireworks). Have students explain the reason for this time lag.

Where Did the Sugar Go?
Physical Science—Dissolving of Crystals in Water
GRADE LEVELS: 4–6

Objectives

- Students generate ideas of what happens to solid crystals as they dissolve in water and determine that large dissolved molecules tend to settle at the bottom of an undisturbed solution.

- Students formulate hypotheses about why dissolving occurs more rapidly when the water is heated or stirred.

National Science Education Standards (National Research Council, 1996) Addressed

All Levels Content Standard A:

- Abilities necessary to do scientific inquiry

Levels K–4 Content Standard B:

- Develop an understanding of properties of objects and materials

Levels 5–8 Content Standard B:

- Develop an understanding of properties and changes of properties in matter

National Educational Technology Standards for Students (NETS·S) Addressed

1. **Creativity and Innovation**

   c. use models and simulations to explore complex systems and issues

   d. identify trends and forecast possibilities

4. **Critical Thinking, Problem Solving, and Decision Making**

   c. collect and analyze data to identify solutions and make informed decisions

Technology/Materials Needed

- Video *Dissolving Sugar Cubes,* downloaded to the computer hard drive from the SITE Screening Room at http://site.aace.org/video/books/teaching/science

- For additional exploration, two other videos from the SITE Screening Room are available: *Sugar in Hot Water* and *Sugar Cubes Stirred*

- Computer and a projector (for a teacher-directed demonstration)

- Computer lab (for direct student use)

CONTENT

The dissolving of a solid in a liquid is an everyday experience with young children. They watch crystals of their favorite fruit drink mix color the water in which it is mixed. They sweeten the drink by putting sugar or sugar substitute crystals in it. But have they really observed what happens to the crystals? The content addressed in this activity is the dissolving of solids in liquids. The students will generate ideas about where the solid sugar crystals go and why.

TECHNOLOGY

Used as a teacher-directed demonstration, all you will need is a computer and a projector. You can start and stop the video as needed and ask questions to promote observation, inference, prediction, and modeling.

For direct student use, a computer lab would be useful. Make sure that the video is stored on the hard drive of each individual computer. If the video is used as an independent activity, students should be given a list of questions to answer as they explore the movie. You can add your own questions, referencing the time code on the movie. For example, you could ask the students to go 30 seconds into the movie to make a specific observation.

PEDAGOGY

Engage

This activity could be done as a live demonstration in the classroom, but the prerecorded time-lapse video allows students to see what happens to the sugar cubes in a short period of time, and the video can be stopped for further directed observation, inference, and predictions.

Before showing the video, tell students to observe carefully as they watch. You may even give them a short list of details to notice. For example, "What was the beginning volume of the water?" (The volume will be stated in the text at the beginning of the movie, or students can look at the graduations on the side of the beaker.) "After the sugar cubes are put in the water, does the volume change?" When possible, students should support their answers throughout this activity with evidence from the video. Now show the video, *Dissolving Sugar Cubes*.

The video includes time-lapse of the sugar dissolving in the water at 25 times normal speed. This feature allows the students to observe subtle changes in the solid and surrounding liquid that may provide clues to the dissolving process. As the video plays, ask students, "Did the level of the water change after the sugar dissolved?" It does not look like the water level is lower in the lower left image of Figure 3.3, but clearly much of the sugar has dissolved by then. Stop the video and ask, "Where did the sugar go, and

FIGURE 3.3. Images from the movie *Dissolving Sugar Cubes.*

how did it get there?" Students should predict where the sugar molecules are located and give some rationale for their reasoning. The next part of the movie will provide a hint. There is no stirring of the solution in this movie. The sugar just dissolves over time.

After the sugar is dissolved, the background of the movie changes to provide a better contrast for the final scene. Food coloring is slowly dropped into the water. The food coloring stays in the upper half of the water. Ask students, "Why might this happen? Where do you think the sugar molecules are located now? What is the mechanism for the solution process? In other words, how did the sugar move from the cube to the liquid?" The students should develop a model for how this process occurred.

As you discuss students' responses after the video, have volunteers come to the computer and move the play-head to the position in the movie that helps them defend their answers. (For example, the upper right image of Figure 3.3 clearly shows that there is an increase in volume.)

Exploration

Ask students, "How would the dissolving rate change if the water was heated before adding the sugar? How would it change if the water was stirred after the sugar was added?" Digital videos that can help answer these questions can also be downloaded from the Screening Room (*Sugar in Hot Water* and *Sugar Cubes Stirred*). When we tested this activity in middle school, students showed the two movies simultaneously to see which movie would win the solution "race." Does this new information support the dissolving model, or does the model need revising?

Analyzing Digital Video Activities

DIGITAL VIDEO can be analyzed in several different ways. A qualitative analysis could include finding patterns, frequency of occurrence, or classification. For example, a video camera could be set up to videotape the activity around a bird's nest for a given hour to count how often the parent bird feeds the young birds. Quantitative analysis includes measurement and relationships among variables and will be the subject of the two activities described in this section. When video is recorded using a consumer-grade digital camera, the images are recorded and played at a rate of approximately 30 images per second. This means that every single image (or "frame") that makes up the motion represents 1/30th of a second. With this information, the digital video can be used as a timer for events. An image sequence of three frames in a video would represent 3/30ths, or 0.10 second. A video with a sequence of 60 frames represents 60/30, or 2.00 seconds. The precision of the timing method is limited to one frame, or 1/30 of a second (approximately 0.03 seconds).

In addition to digital video being used as a timing tool, software tools currently available enable students to measure the motion captured on digital video. If the captured video includes an object of known length that is equidistant from the video camera as the event being captured, distance measurements can be made. Data from that measurement along with the frame rate enables the calculation of velocity and acceleration. If masses of the objects captured in the video are known, momentum, energy, and forces can also be determined.

Measuring the Speed of Sound
Physics–Sound
GRADE LEVELS: 9–12

Objectives

▪ Students accurately analyze the speed of sound by using the frame rate of the digital video.

National Science Education Standards (National Research Council, 1996) Addressed

All Levels Content Standard A:

▪ Abilities necessary to do scientific inquiry

Levels 5–8 Content Standard B:

▪ Develop an understanding of the transfer of energy

Levels 9–12 Content Standard B:

▪ Develop an understanding of interactions of energy and matter

National Educational Technology Standards for Students (NETS·S) Addressed

1. **Creativity and Innovation**

    d. identify trends and forecast possibilities

3. **Research and Information Fluency**

    b. locate, organize, analyze, evaluate, synthesize, and ethically use information from a variety of sources and media

    d. process data and report results

4. **Critical Thinking, Problem Solving, and Decision Making**

    c. collect and analyze data to identify solutions and make informed decisions

Technology/Materials Needed

▪ Video clips downloaded from the SITE Screening Room (http://site.aace.org/video/books/teaching/science) before beginning the activity:

   ▪ *Speed of Sound II*

   ▪ *Speed of Sound at 210 Meters*

   ▪ *Measuring Time Differences Using iMovie6*

▪ You may also want students to analyze the additional videos from the SITE Screening Room:

   ▪ *Fireworks Burst 1*

   ▪ *Fireworks Burst 2*

CONTENT

The speed of sound can be found in a variety of ways. The most straightforward way for middle and high school students to calculate the speed of sound is to use the same method to determine the average velocity of a moving object. If the distance traveled and the required time of travel is known, the average velocity is calculated by change in distance divided by change in time. However, since the speed of sound is quite fast, the distance needs to be long, and timing needs to be more precise than can be accomplished using a human activated stopwatch for an accurate calculation.

TECHNOLOGY

In order to easily analyze differences in audio events in the digital video, the software you use needs to have the capability to show the audio amplitude in the audio track so students can determine when the major sound events occurred. If you have access to Macintosh computers, use iMovie with this activity. It is free software that comes with Mac computers. In order to expedite student work, the necessary video clips should be placed into the iMovie file and labeled so students will know which clip is for which distance. This file should be stored on any computer on which the analysis will be done.

The time delay on the video may also be measured on both Mac and PC computers using Vernier Logger Pro, with a microphone probe connected into the LabPro interface and connected to the computer. Detailed instructions for this method can be found in the *Measuring Time Differences Using iMovie6* video.

PEDAGOGY

Explore and Explain

Before beginning this activity, you may want to go through the activity using the digital movie *Speed of Sound II*, which is described in the Watching Digital Video Activities section of this chapter.

After providing an introduction, have students watch the unedited video clip *Speed of Sound at 210 Meters* using iMovie or equivalent software. Students should extract the sound and measure the time difference between the sound heard through the two-way radio and the sound traveling through the air. The method for finding time differences is found in the digital video *Measuring Time Differences Using iMovie6*.

In the case of 210 meters distance, the time difference between the two sounds is 18 frames, or 0.594 seconds. Therefore, the calculated average velocity is 210 meters / 0.594 seconds = 354 meters per second. This is relatively close to the accepted value, knowing that the uncertainty of the timing measurement is one-half frame out of 18 frames.

Clips from other distances can be used, but there should be a discussion of how the errors could increase greatly if the distances are too short. For example, at a distance of 60 meters, it takes about five frames for the sound to travel from Preston to the camera. One-half frame uncertainty out of five frames is 10%.

Students should think about other questions while doing this activity. For example, "When looking at the audio track from iMovie, the sound waveform from the radio seems to have a different appearance than the sound waveform through the air. Why might this be the case?" To eliminate the radio speaker as a possible source of explanation, students could look at the sound pattern when the noise is generated near the camera. Students might also consider the following question: "Based on the average results of the average speed of sound in air, would you say the day the video was shot was a hot day or a cool day? What other information would be needed to answer this question?"

Elaboration

In the elaboration stage, students use explanations and skills in a new but similar situation. Students can use their knowledge of the speed of sound to determine how far away a noisy event occurs. For example, two fireworks displays were videotaped at different distances from the launch site (*Fireworks Burst 1* and *Fireworks Burst 2*). Using the described timing techniques students can view the videos and determine the time between the bursts and sound of the bursts. By knowing the speed of sound at the temperature the scenes were shot, the students can calculate the distance of the camera from the bursts (Figure 3.4).

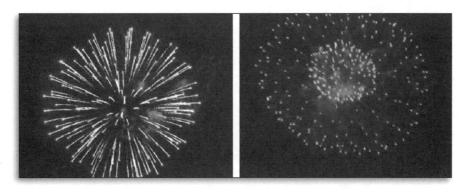

FIGURE 3.4. Images of two fireworks bursts videotaped from different distances.

Analysis of the Motion of a Model Rocket
Physics—Velocity and Acceleration
GRADE LEVELS: 10–12

Objectives

- Students measure the motion using frame-by-frame analysis of the position of a model rocket.

- Students generate possible reasons for the changes in velocity during the flight of the rocket.

National Science Education Standards (National Research Council, 1996) Addressed

All Levels Content Standard A:

- Abilities necessary to do scientific inquiry

Levels 9–12 Content Standard B:

- Develop an understanding of motions and forces

National Educational Technology Standards for Students (NETS·S) Addressed

1. **Creativity and Innovation**

    d. identify trends and forecast possibilities

3. **Research and Information Fluency**

    b. locate, organize, analyze, evaluate, synthesize, and ethically use information from a variety of sources and media

    d. process data and report results

4. **Critical Thinking, Problem Solving, and Decision Making**

    c. collect and analyze data to identify solutions and make informed decisions

5. **Digital Citizenship**

    b. exhibit a positive attitude toward using technology that supports collaboration, learning, and productivity

Technology/Materials Needed

- Videos downloaded from the SITE Screening Room (http://site.aace.org/video/books/teaching/science):

    - *SR-71 Blackbird*

    - *Motion Analysis Using Logger Pro*

- Motion analysis software

CONTENT

Several variables can influence the motion of a launched model rocket, including the magnitude of the force acting on the rocket and the mass of the rocket. In order to study the effects of these variables on the rocket's motion, one must be able to describe and quantify the motion of the rocket. The known frame rate of the video can be used to determine the velocity of the rocket throughout the entire flight if the position of the rocket on the video frame can be measured and if a reference distance is known.

TECHNOLOGY

In addition to the prerecorded digital video, you will need motion analysis software. The software used in this example is Vernier Logger Pro, but there are several commercial packages available for this task, as well as shareware software.

Students should work on individual computers with this activity. Practice using the software will allow the students to construct their ideas about the effects of force on change of motion. The questions within the activity serve as an impetus for guided inquiry. You could do the activity as a demonstration with a computer and projector, but students may not be as active in the construction of their own knowledge if you use this strategy.

PEDAGOGY

Exploration

Using the digital video *SR-71 Blackbird*, students will flip through a series of images, noting the change of position of a rocket in each frame of the movie. The longer the distance the object travels during subsequent frames, the faster it is traveling. Expand the movie so it is large on the screen. Click through the movie one frame at a time. Note that the rocket does not lift off the launch pad in the first frame that smoke is observed. Based on change in position for each subsequent frame, where do you think the rocket is moving the fastest?

Explanation

Successive calculations of velocity will enable the student to determine a change in velocity (acceleration). Through the use of graphical analysis, students will be able to determine the relative size and direction of the forces acting on the rocket during various stages of flight. Students will construct the idea that acceleration is determined from the slope of a line in a velocity-time graph.

Although students could display the digital movie onto a whiteboard and plot positions of the rocket in subsequent frames to visualize the change in motion of the rocket, for more rapid data collection, they should use motion analysis software. After students mark the positions of the rocket, the computer will calculate the distance and velocity of the rocket

FIGURE 3.5. Nate stands beside the launch pad ready to ignite the engine.

for each frame or set of frames and plot the results automatically on a velocity-time graph. Students will interpret the resulting graph.

Two pieces of information are needed before the analysis can be accomplished: (a) the frame rate of the digital video and (b) the height of an object that is equidistant from the camera lens as the object for motion measurement. The frame rate of this video we will use is the standard 30 frames per second. Figure 3.5 is an image of the event just before the rocket is launched.

Introduce the video by telling students that the rocket chosen for this activity was painted black. The white engine smoke will serve as good contrast with the ground and trees, and the black rocket will contrast well with the light blue sky. A rocket of relatively large mass and an engine that had low impulse (A8-3) was chosen so the entire flight could be captured while keeping the camera motionless. The student is 5.5 feet tall.

After the movie is imported into the software, students should set the origin and use the height of the student as a reference length. Data collection begins. As students click on the rocket, the video advances to the next frame. With each click of the button on the rocket image, the position is measured and velocity is calculated and plotted on the graph. This process continues until the user decides to end the data collection. Students may decide not to use all of the frames if the motion is relatively slow across the screen. They can use every third frame or some other interval that makes the data collection easier.

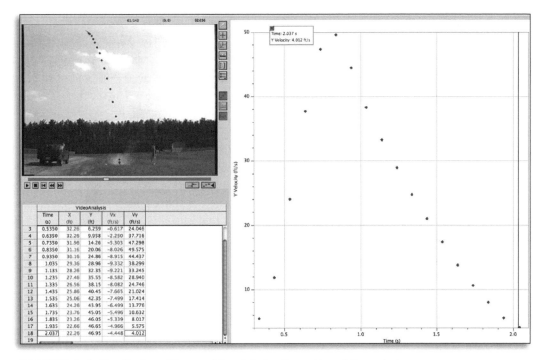

	Time (s)	X (ft)	Y (ft)	Vx (ft/s)	Vy (ft/s)
3	0.5350	32.26	6.259	-0.617	24.046
4	0.6350	32.26	9.958	-2.250	37.716
5	0.7350	31.96	14.26	-5.303	47.298
6	0.8350	31.16	20.06	-8.026	49.575
7	0.9350	30.16	24.86	-8.915	44.437
8	1.035	29.36	28.96	-9.332	38.299
9	1.135	28.26	32.35	-9.221	33.245
10	1.235	27.46	35.55	-8.582	28.940
11	1.335	26.56	38.15	-8.082	24.746
12	1.435	25.86	40.45	-7.665	21.024
13	1.535	25.06	42.35	-7.499	17.414
14	1.635	24.26	43.95	-6.499	13.776
15	1.735	23.76	45.05	-5.496	10.632
16	1.835	23.26	46.05	-5.339	8.017
17	1.935	22.66	46.65	-4.966	5.575
18	2.037	22.26	46.95	-4.448	4.012
19					

FIGURE 3.6. The display of the resulting data for the motion of the rocket.

An example of the resulting data collection and data presentation is shown in Figure 3.6. In this example, every third frame was used for data collection. See the digital video *Motion Analysis Using Logger Pro* to view a step-by-step demonstration of this analysis.

As students examine the data and scroll across the graph, the corresponding frames of the digital video are displayed, showing the position of the rocket. The first five data points on the graph show a rapid increase in velocity, changing from about 5 ft/s to a maximum of around 50 ft/s. Students should answer the question "What is the position of the rocket when it hits its maximum velocity?" To answer that question, they can scroll across the graph to the maximum velocity and then look at the video. The movie shows the rocket just clearing the tree line. Ask, "Why does the velocity increase during that period of time (0 to 0.835 seconds)? Why does the velocity decrease after that point?"

To find out how high the rocket was at maximum velocity, students taking high school physics can find the area under the velocity-time curve. To do this, they point and drag from time 0 to time 0.835 seconds, and select the integrate icon. The area under this portion of the velocity-time curve is 15 feet.

Help students note that the greatest slope of the graph is at the beginning of the launch. Using the linear fit tool for these selected points, students can find that the slope has a magnitude of 120 ft/s/s. Ask, "What forces are acting on the rocket at this time? Which force is the greatest?"

Just after the rocket reaches its maximum velocity, the slope of the line represents a change of velocity of -56 ft/s/s, but toward the end of the collected data, the change in velocity is only -25 ft/s/s. Ask, "What forces are acting on the rocket after the engine stops? Why is there a difference between the two measured slopes after the engine stops?" Figure 3.7 displays the same graph when investigating both distance and change of velocity (acceleration) at various points of the flight.

The motion analysis software is not necessary for the analysis of the digital video. However, without the software students will spend much time measuring video distances, converting those distances to actual distances, calculating average velocity between sequential frames, and plotting each of those points with respect to time. Students could decrease this effort if they had knowledge of spreadsheet calculations. If the objective is to have students learn to calculate velocity and construct velocity-time graphs, this methodology would be fine. The time may be better spent on the analysis of the resulting graph, not computing values for the points on the graph.

MODIFICATION

If you have the proper equipment and the outdoor space to try it, students can film their own rocket flights for analysis.

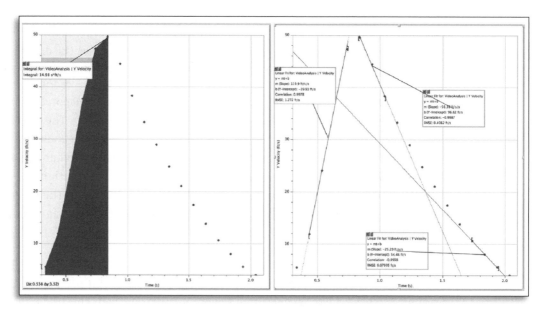

FIGURE 3.7. Finding distance and acceleration using the integral and slope options.

Creating Digital Video Activity

LEARNING SCIENCE can happen while capturing and editing video of events that depict science concepts. Students should be encouraged either to assist the teacher in shooting and editing the video or to create their own digital video of events in which they are interested. For example, the dissolving sugar cubes described earlier in the chapter were recorded to get students to think about the mechanism by which sugar dissolves. After the video was edited to simulate time-lapse photography, we noticed that there was increased refraction of light by the liquid in the bottom of the beaker, which promoted further exploration. This led to the discovery that the concentration of the sugar solution was not the same throughout the water in the beaker, which prompted the use of food coloring to show this situation. Both you and your students can explore and test ideas as the footage is captured.

As indicated by the proliferation of video being uploaded to websites such as YouTube, students want to be seen by others. Thoughts that dominate the adolescent mind include "look at me" and "look at what I can do." Using this as motivation, we can encourage students to be the star in events that display concepts in science. Students can create movies to express their knowledge of a specific event. They can record on video events for which they have no explanation, but use the medium to challenge others to figure out why the events happened as they did. They can also stage an event for others to collect data, find patterns, and generate predictions. Creating digital video also allows students to practice their science process skills. One such skill is often overlooked at the late elementary levels: the process skill of modeling. The next example focuses on that process skill.

Modeling the Solar Eclipse
Earth/Space Science—Motion of the Moon
GRADE LEVELS: 4–6

Objective

- Students demonstrate a solar eclipse, illustrating the effect of observer distance on the apparent size of the sun and moon.

National Science Education Standards (National Research Council, 1996) Addressed

All Levels Content Standard A:

- Abilities necessary to do scientific inquiry

Levels K–4 Content Standard D:

- Develop an understanding of properties of objects in the sky and changes in earth and sky

Levels 5–8 Content Standard D:

- Develop an understanding of Earth in the solar system

National Educational Technology Standards for Students (NETS·S) Addressed

1. **Creativity and Innovation**

    b. create original works as a means of personal or group expression

2. **Communication and Collaboration**

    a. interact, collaborate, and publish with peers, experts, or others employing a variety of digital environments and media

    d. contribute to project teams to produce original works or solve problems

3. **Research and Information Fluency**

    a. plan strategies to guide inquiry

4. **Critical Thinking, Problem Solving, and Decision Making**

    b. plan and manage activities to develop a solution or complete a project

Technology/Materials Needed

- Book or prescreened websites with information on the relative size and position of the sun and the moon with respect to the Earth

- *Modeling the Solar Eclipse*—video found on the SITE Screening Room at http://site.aace.org/video/books/teaching/science/

- Digital video camera with a tripod and a way to do simple editing of raw video footage

CONTENT

Students are well aware of the periodic patterns that are everyday experiences. For example, they notice that the sun is what provides daylight. They may notice that the moon looks different at different times of the month and that it can be seen during the day and during the night. Observation of the motion of the sun and the moon can enable students to see these periodic patterns of location and appearance. Although students may note the appearance, few understand the reasons for it.

An eclipse is a most difficult problem for those who have an egocentric point of view: they need to look outside of their own visual reference frame to fully understand why the eclipse is happening and why only certain people on the Earth can view the eclipse as it happens. For this activity, the students are asked to model a solar eclipse and videotape the model from a position that represents the observers' location.

TECHNOLOGY

Students will need to search out information regarding the relative size and position of the sun and the moon with respect to the Earth. They could either look for this information in a book, or they could review prescreened websites that provide the information. The advantage of the use of websites is that they may also provide simulations of the motion of the moon around the Earth. This information would serve as an advanced organizer for the activity.

The video *Modeling the Solar Eclipse* (found on the SITE Screening Room at http://site.aace.org/video/books/teaching/science) will also be useful.

Other technology requirements would be a digital video camera with a tripod and a method to do some simple editing of the raw video footage. For example, students may make some alignment errors in the video, or they may stumble with some of the words they used. These clips should not be used in their final cut of the video.

PEDAGOGY

Present students with the following task:

You are to demonstrate the total eclipse of the sun using common materials that can be found around a home. You will videotape and edit your demonstration. A portion of the video must include the blocking from view of one object by a second object as seen from the video camera. Try to model the total eclipse of the sun as accurately as possible.

The class should be divided into groups of three to four students. One video should be produced from each group's effort. Give students the opportunity to search for

FIGURE 3.8. Images from *Modeling the Solar Eclipse* illustrating how a smaller object can obscure a larger object.

information regarding the Earth, moon, and sun. Also, give them guiding questions that may or may not be modeled within the assigned video, such as:

■ Does the moon follow the same path around the Earth as viewed from the sun at various times of the year?

■ How does the moon's distance from the Earth influence how much area can be eclipsed?

■ Why can the eclipse be seen from some locations of the Earth and not others?

■ Can the solar eclipse be seen during the night?

Students should be able to answer these questions by physically modeling the situation, using a video camera as the point of view from Earth or from the sun. It may take some tweaking of object size and distances. The orbit could be modeled by a string tied to a stopper that revolves around the Earth and the camera placed at the sun's viewpoint. A representative model of the moon could be moved different distances away from the Earth to see the effect of distance on eclipse area. A camera viewing a model of the eclipsed sun could be shifted slightly to one direction to show a partial eclipse, or even no eclipse, depending on the shift distance. The camera could point away from the model of the sun (representing night) to answer the fourth question.

After the students create models to answer the guiding questions, they can create their own video that would communicate how solar eclipses occur. Nate's group decided to begin their video by showing how his head can completely obscure a large window when he is near the camera, while the next scene shows him standing beside the window, which is clearly larger than his head (view *Modeling the Solar Eclipse* in the SITE Screening Room). Using this size versus distance idea, he continues the model showing how a golf ball can completely obscure the much larger basketball (Figure 3.8).

FIGURE 3.9. Screen shots from *Modeling the Solar Eclipse* illustrating the relative motion of the moon during a solar eclipse.

Later in the video, Nate models the motion of the moon across the sun (Figure 3.9). Note that the general direction of the motion is correct, although the path of the moon's travel across the sun is usually more of an angle.

This activity allows students to take an abstract phenomenon and make it into a concrete model that they can understand. Guiding questions for student exploration are essential for accurate understanding of the solar eclipse.

Conclusion

LITERATURE ON the use of video in exploring science reveals that short, single-concept digital video can be effective in the teaching of science concepts. The intent of this chapter was to focus on noncommercial digital video products than can be used in the science classroom and laboratory to promote science process skills of students. Use teacher- and student-generated videos on websites such as the SITE Screening Room, Teacher Tube, or YouTube for watching and analyzing. Create flexible-format digital videos that can be posted to such venues that will enable other teachers to use what you have successfully developed and tested. Become a part of the Web 2.0 culture to enhance the learning of science through digital video.

> **MAKING VIDEOS**
>
> See Chapter 6, "Acquiring Digital Video," for more about making your own videos for teaching and learning science.

References

American Association for the Advancement of Science. (1965). *Science: A process approach commentary for teachers.* Washington, DC: Author.

Bybee, R. W., Powell, J. C., & Trowbridge, L. W. (2008). *Teaching secondary school science.* Columbus, OH: Pearson.

Fuller, R. G. (Ed.). (2002). *A love of discovery: Science education, the second career of Robert Karplus.* New York, NY: Kluwer Academic.

International Society for Technology in Education. (2007). *National educational technology standards for students* (2nd ed.). Eugene, OR: Author.

Karplus, R., & Thier, H. (1967). *A new look at elementary school science.* Chicago, IL: Rand McNally.

Lawson, A. E., Abraham, M. R., & Renner, J. W. (1989). *A theory of instruction: Using the Learning Cycle to teach science concepts and thinking skills.* Cincinnati, OH: National Association for Research in Science Teaching.

National Research Council. (1996). *National science education standards.* Washington, DC: National Academies Press.

CHAPTER 4

Sara B. Kajder and
Carl A. Young

digital video in
English language arts education

THIS IS both a daunting and an exhilarating time to teach English. The core components of our field—reading, writing, literacy, text, and community—are shifting. Alongside rapid changes in everyday literacy practices outside of our classrooms, students enter school multiply literate, whereas curricula remain largely focused on print-based texts. Students learn these multiple, 21st-century literacies mostly without our instruction: reading and writing online with purpose for a variety of defined audiences, using their own choice of tools, and achieving tangible outcomes and relevance. New technologies and the literacies they make possible create a time of risk and possibility, opening up new modes and media for communication—and creating new opportunities for what teaching English really means.

In order to consider the role of digital video in the English classroom, we must start by exploring the possibilities opened by new literacies theory, broadly differing definitions of what constitutes a "text," and the varied means and modes supporting multimodal compositions. These shifts come at a time when the technologies we can potentially access are marked by new thinking: focusing on a collective intelligence, expertise that is distributed and collective, value as a function of dispersion, and tools that make possible a different, global approach to mediating and relating. Media is creative, but we also are now provided with an opportunity to use media to do things—to create, produce, manipulate, and share evolving conceptions of text and multimedia products.

Text, New Literacies, and Multimodality

DIGITAL TOOLS make possible new kinds of text. Our definition of the term is expanding well past print-based texts. "Text is not restricted to written prose; text can be primarily visual, such as an animated graphic, video clip, photo slideshow, or image with little accompanying verbal information, and verbal information presented in an auditory rather than written format" (Dalton & Proctor, 2008, p. 301).

With this expanded definition, teachers of English must now aid students in making meaning within and across a range of multimodal texts. To complicate this work further, new texts require new teaching strategies to engage students' understanding. Where new tools have often been fitted into traditional classroom work (e.g., typing a paper in a word processor), new texts require new ways of reading and comprehending, new strategies for composing, and new pairings for intertextual study as students read across a range of media and texts.

The "new" in new literacies refers to the rapid changes in technologies that now make literacy more about knowing which tool, mode, and media form is best for accomplishing a given task. "New literacies will continuously be new, multiple, and rapidly disseminated" (Coiro, Knobel, Lankshear, & Leu, 2008, p. 5). By definition, a continual tension is established between "new" and "known"—a tension in direct opposition with stable, print-centric literacies. Teaching becomes more about learning. Teachers are positioned to explore continually how to make meaning of, and how to produce texts in, multiple modes (e.g., visual, print, digital, multimodal, kinesthetic) and how those texts mediate our understandings of literacy.

In doing so, we co-construct literacy practices with students, creating learning opportunities both more mutual and more authentic. As O'Brien (2006) points out, "It is impossible to say this is literacy now, rather, we must constantly retool, redefine, and figure out what to attend to during the evolution" (p. 43). In effect, literacy in the 21st century requires an ability to constantly adapt to and apply emerging technologies.

Although older forms of video may have been used in schools to varying degrees, digital video enters into the English classroom as a new media form and a new tool for multimodal composition. Research is, at best, still emerging when it comes to examining the role of digital video in the English language arts classroom, but we know that students learn best when they use multiliteracies to read and compose in new ways. Further, integrating visual images with written text, as done in most digital stories and multimodal compositions, enhances and accelerates comprehension. Meaning, here, is not necessarily additive. Text and pictures often say more when juxtaposed, and the effect is further amplified when motion, design, and interactivity are added.

Composing with digital video—creating digital stories, book trailers, music videos, screencasts, and more—requires an examination of how we produce, distribute, invent, explore, persuade, and create impact with texts written for specific audiences. Composing with digital video alongside Web 2.0 tools enables opportunities for leveraging audience participation for authentic collaboration and feedback. Writing with multimedia tools is a process of linking message and tool, purpose and audience—while actively critiquing the very tools used for expressing meaning.

Students who write with multimodal tools (such as digital video editors) do so selectively and intentionally, and they leverage the unique capacities of the tools and media in order to accomplish a specific goal. As in print-centric writing tasks, the principles of choice and form matter, as does the larger context in which the writing is situated. To be fully literate, students must know how to use tools, but more importantly, they must know which forms of literacy will best support their purpose for a given audience and a specific context.

Bringing Together the New and Known: Digital Video and Film Studies

FILM STUDIES has often been a part of the English curriculum, typically taught as a tool for leading students to more deeply consider particular works of literature or to inspire composition. We study film as an art form. We study its literary elements, cinematography (e.g., specific terms for camera angles or shots, editing, or special effects), and the dramatic/performance elements it captures.

Digital video repositories now put a variety of films into circulation, but film study is not what we are discussing in this chapter. The distinction here is important. Twenty-first-century tools afford students new possibilities as active learners. We are asking students to use digital video to make critical connections to content and process learning. We are also suggesting that they use digital video to create artifacts of learning, artifacts that will serve as a channel for expressive and analytical thought, as a means for engaging with an authentic audience, and as a tool for developing readers, writers, thinkers, speakers, listeners, and viewers.

The activities that follow leverage the unique capacities of digital video, following the anchoring scaffold of watch, analyze, and create. We define each of these in specific ways that are central to our discipline and that might vary from other chapters in this book. Given the statement on 21st-century learning issued by the National Council of Teachers of English (2008), the National Council of Teachers of English standards (International Reading Association and NCTE, 1996), the ISTE National Educational Technology Standards for Students (NETS·S, 2007), and the criteria used by the Partnership for 21st Century Skills (2008), we use the scaffold of watch/analyze/create in the following ways:

Watch. Separate from the conventional idea of film studies in the English classroom (where we might watch a film after reading a literary text), watching, here, is about active meaning-making and then using response to accomplish a specific task. For example, we might ask students to watch a collection of short videos from the Folger Shakespeare Library to examine performance, but we do so with an eye on informing students' performance and literary interpretation. Watching video requires that teachers answer the question, "We are viewing this in order to do what?"

Analyze. Analysis of video in this context centers on the skills of evaluating the multiple layers of the multimodal text/digital video, examining the literary impact of the pairing of spoken words/print text/soundtrack/image/motion. We borrow from the kinds of analytical skills used when working with print texts (e.g., novels, plays, poetry), and we expand the question set to explore each of the modes singularly and in interaction with one another, where meaning is multiplicative. As with watching, the work does not stop with the completion of the analysis (in writing or discussion). The analysis is used to fuel additional work.

Create. Here, students apply their knowledge of multimodal composition to create a text, sometimes in response to a specific prompt, but always in an attempt to express, to communicate specific ideas by intentionally pairing specific modes of communicating, and to connect with an identified audience.

The selected pedagogical themes of this book—watch, analyze, and create—provide insights into ways to maximize the potential of digital video as an instructional tool. In the three sections addressing these categories, detailed examples of ways digital video can be used in the English language arts classroom are included. Through these examples, we aim to highlight the potential of digital video for enhancing the context of rich content learning and authentic pedagogical settings. Each activity will address the actions of the students, as well as the ways in which you can use digital video to bridge into, enhance, or support content learning and engage students in critical thinking, thus, avoiding passive instances of student engagement (or lack thereof).

Watching, Analyzing, and Creating Digital Video

THIS CHAPTER has three digital video activities:

WATCHING DIGITAL VIDEO IN LANGUAGE ARTS

- ▪ *Northern Exposure* Clips–Bridging into Inquiry

ANALYZING DIGITAL VIDEO IN LANGUAGE ARTS

- ▪ Performance Poetry

CREATING DIGITAL VIDEO IN LANGUAGE ARTS

- ▪ Digital Book Trailers

As these activities will demonstrate, there is some blurring across each of the three categories, as students might first need to create a digital video before moving to analysis. It is entirely possible that such analysis would then fuel creation. We do not mean these to be listed in any sequential order or to reflect a tiered depth, sophistication, or rigor of task.

CONTENT STANDARDS

The English Language Arts Standards are sponsored by the National Council of Teachers of English and the International Reading Association, www.ncte.org/about/over/standards.

Northern Exposure Clips—
Bridging into Inquiry
Watching Digital Video in Language Arts
GRADE LEVELS: 7–12

Objective

■   Students will be able to use prior knowledge to develop their own inquiry projects.

National Council of Teachers of English/International Reading Association Standards (1996) Addressed

5.   Students employ a wide range of strategies as they write and use different writing process elements appropriately to communicate with different audiences for a variety of purposes

8.   Students use a variety of technological and information resources (e.g., libraries, databases, computer networks, video) to gather and synthesize information and to create and communicate knowledge

National Educational Technology Standards for Students (NETS•S) Addressed

2.   **Communication and Collaboration**

   a.   interact, collaborate, and publish with peers, experts, or others employing a variety of digital environments and media

   c.   develop cultural understanding and global awareness by engaging with learners of other cultures

   d.   contribute to project teams to produce original works or solve problems

4.   **Critical Thinking, Problem Solving, and Decision Making**

   a.   identify and define authentic problems and significant questions for investigation

   b.   plan and manage activities to develop a solution or complete a project

Technology/Materials Needed

■   "The Final Frontier" (Season 3, Episode 20) from *Northern Exposure*. (If you are showing the episode clips on a DVD player, you can fast-forward and pause as needed according to the times provided for each clip. If you are showing the film via a media player such as Windows Media Player, you can move the cursor to the appropriate starting times.)

CONTENT

The content focus in this activity is on getting students to better understand human nature and the connection between how we learn as human beings and authentic inquiry. Judith Wells Lindfors (1999) wrote, "I believe that inquiry is universal, a part of what it is to be human." Students can engage in various activities exploring the nature of curiosity and inquiry, including watching selected clips from an episode of the television show *Northern Exposure* entitled "The Final Frontier." In this episode, a mysterious package arrives in Cicely, Alaska, covered with stamps from around the world. The townspeople face their curiosities about the package and decide what to do with it: either send it to the dead-parcel branch in San Francisco, where authorized postal personnel claim the package, or open it themselves to see what is inside.

TECHNOLOGY

If you are showing the *Northern Exposure* episode clips on a DVD player, you can fast-forward and pause as needed according to the times provided for each clip. If you are showing the film via a media player such as Windows Media Player, you can move the cursor to the appropriate starting times:

- First clip (0:30:10–0:33:05)

- Second clip (0:36:31–0:38:20)

- Third clip (0:39:44–0:40:55)

PEDAGOGY

Prior to showing the video clips from the *Northern Exposure* episode, have students compose a guided freewrite of reactions to, understanding of, or associations with the following aphorism:

"Curiosity killed the cat."

After 3 to 4 minutes, have some of the students share and discuss some of their responses, including the general sense here that the quotation serves as a warning about curiosity. Then, have them freewrite again addressing a related quotation:

"Where there is curiosity, a mouse may be caught."

Again, have students discuss their responses, including juxtaposing the two quotations. Guide students to consider the two quotations as a representation of ideas about how human beings learn. On the one hand, curiosity is presented as a dangerous option, perhaps one to be avoided. Thus, learning is passive: we take information in from others and safely repeat it. The second quotation represents the other end of the spectrum, where curiosity becomes a metaphor for learning itself. It has much more positive connotations about what our innate curiosity yields—unless, of course, you are the mouse!

Next, engage students in a discussion about where they see themselves on this continuum represented by the quotations and how they perceive curiosity and its

FIGURE 4.1. Do the citizens of Cicely have the authority to open
the package?

connections to humans and the ways we learn? Have students consider how they learned
as infants and continued to learn as they grew older. Typically, infants learn by exploring
their environments, engaging their curiosity, mimicking and mirroring what they see
others doing, and trial and error. Over time, this natural curiosity often is mediated by
authority figures who dispense knowledge with the expectation that it will be memorized
and accessible later for quizzes and tests. Explain that although this is one approach to
learning and the nature of knowing, inquiry provides another approach—a more active
one. It holds the potential for each of us to create knowledge ourselves. Show the video
clips from *Northern Exposure* as a bridge to having students engage in their own inquiry
activity.

The first clip (0:30:10–0:33:05) features a town hall meeting in which the citizens of
Cicely are presented with the dilemma of what to do with a mysterious package that has
arrived in town without an addressee. The sender is a Richard McWilliams, who is not
one of the 215 town residents, and the package contains stamps from all over the world.
Ruth-Anne, the town's postmistress, calls a meeting to get consensus on whether to open
the package. The town doctor, Joel Fleishman, questions whether they have the authority
to open the package (Figure 4.1).

Ruth-Anne explains that they don't, technically, and that the package, if still unclaimed
after 15 days, should be sent to the dead-parcel branch in San Francisco to be opened by
authorized personnel. Because it will be opened anyway, some argue that they should
open it. Joel takes a stand promoting the "sanctity" of the U.S. mail and advocates not
opening the package. Chris, the town radio DJ and philosopher/theologian, argues that
the stamps are more than just "bureaucratic hieroglyphics" and represent a "sacred

trust," comparing the opening of the package to the great personal risk involved in opening King Tut's tomb.

After a short, dramatic pause, Marilyn Whirlwind dryly replies, "I'll take that risk," inspiring a large portion of the townsfolk to applaud and take her side. Chris then enthusiastically chimes in and explains the nature of Marilyn's stance as "the other side of the coin, the bane and blessing of human nature, that old cat killer, curiosity. Something so deeply imbedded in our psyches that it screams to us from ancient myths of Pandora, Eve, Lot's wife—"

Joel interjects at this point, asserting, "Eve lost paradise; Lot's wife was turned into a pillar of salt!" To which Chris responds, "Hey, knowledge doesn't come cheap my friend. Good or bad, curiosity is woven into our DNA like tonsils or opposable thumbs. It's the fire under the ass of the human experience!"

> **WARNING**
>
> This *Northern Exposure* episode contains the word *ass*. As with all digital video material you present, determine beforehand if the language is suitable for your class.

The rhetoric continues. By the end of the clip, the crowd is won, and it's clear that Marilyn's motion will carry.

As a way of engaging students viewing experience, have them consider the following questions as they watch:

- What is the dilemma facing the citizens of Cicely?

- What are the positions presented during the town hall meeting about what to do with the mysterious package? How are those positions supported?

- What are some of the historical, religious, and mythological allusions presented in this clip? What effects do they create or have on the audience?

- Where do you stand in terms of the positions presented? In other words, what do you think should be done about the package, and how might this fit with your sense of human nature?

- What do you think is in the package? Why?

After viewing this initial clip, have students discuss the experience by answering some of these questions. Use the clip and discussion to bridge into a related inquiry-based learning assignment in which you want to engage students. The content might be focused or more open-ended. Provide students with the option to explore topics of genuine interest to them that they negotiate with you. The inquiry strategy you employ might

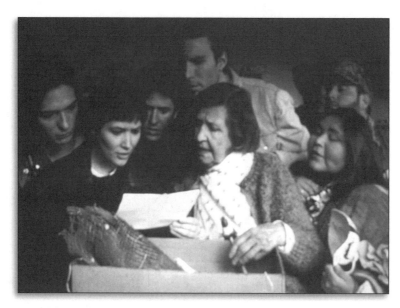

FIGURE 4.2. The citizens of Cicely satisfy their curiosity.

be an I-Search paper, a multi-genre research project, or an oral history assignment. You could consider having students create a digital video as a product of their findings.

At some point during their inquiry process, you can follow up the initial video clip with two additional short clips that follow this story line: one that reveals what the towns-people found in the box once they opened it (0:36:31–0:38:20), and one that focuses on their response to what they find (0:39:44–0:40:55, Figure 4.2).

As it turns out, Richard McWilliams is an 8-year-old, as indicated by his letter inside the box. His letter explains that his family is going to a lake for summer vacation. He wanted to go to Antarctica instead, but his mother said they didn't have the time or money. Richard sent his letter and box with the hope that it would go to all of the places he wanted to go but could not. He requests that recipients put something in the box that represents their particular place. Upon opening the box, the townsfolk find that the box contains artifacts from all of the different places to which the package has been mailed so far. The last clip focuses on what the folks from Cicely decide to add to it and where they will mail it next.

After viewing the last two clips, you can engage students in a discussion of how they might make their own inquiry projects accessible to others beyond the classroom. While mailing them has a certain Flat Stanley appeal, the *Northern Exposure* episode predates the rise of the Internet and all of the possibilities it provides for students to make connections virtually, as well as to access and post artifacts online. Being able to collaborate with other students virtually across the state, country, or globe is another option in terms of collaborative inquiry and sharing research findings.

MORE IDEAS FOR WATCHING DIGITAL VIDEO IN LANGUAGE ARTS

- *Watch screencasts of writers' peer reviews.* Following a process approach to writing, students run through a cycle of messy drafts, which attempt to get closer to what they mean to express, sometimes by inserting or deleting ideas from notes and comments from peer readers. As readers of student writing, teachers read the student essay, read the student writer, and read ourselves as teachers. This is hard work, and it is work we expect students to do when we ask them to provide comments while peer-reviewing another students' work. One way to expand our options is to collaborate with other classrooms through participatory media such as wikis. Students can use screencast software to create a visual and auditory mini-movie that documents their work as peer reviewers. The mini-movie also provides each writer with a multimodal text capturing both what the reader understood the draft to be saying and how the reader moved through the paper, as reflected in the notes, embedded comments, highlighting, and other "moves" captured in the visual component of the screencast. If students work with peers in another school, the screencast has particular relevance in terms of a genuine purpose and authentic audience.

- *Juxtapose print texts with digital video adaptations.* Many literary works have been transformed into film adaptations. Students can benefit from considering how film and digital video enhance the study of literature and vice versa, especially in terms of juxtaposing directorial and authorial technique. For example, Ambrose Bierce's Civil War–focused short story, "An Occurrence at Owl Creek Bridge," has been adapted into at least four short film adaptations. One recasts the story in World War II, focusing on a French resistance fighter fleeing from German soldiers, while another, a French adaptation directed by Robert Enrico, stays truer to the Civil War setting. Enrico's adaptation is particularly compelling, especially in the dramatic way dialogue is purposely, strategically omitted. It won awards at Cannes in 1962 and at the Academy Awards in 1963, and it aired as an episode of *The Twilight Zone*. It is available on DVD and is accessible online in three parts on YouTube. There is no shortage of literary texts that have been translated into film; the key is appropriately scaffolding the watching process and then having students juxtapose the print and video versions.

- *Watch dramatic adaptations.* Allowing your students to watch a film adaptation in class while reading the text can greatly enhance their understanding of the text, as well as heighten their emotional response to it. With plays, especially, the focus is on the spoken word. For example, Shakespearean drama can be made much more accessible and comprehensible to students when the language is further clarified and contextualized through visuals, gestures, props, settings, and action. In effect, the film versions allow students to fill gaps in their comprehension of the text and better understand the context, subtext, and atmosphere of a play. Again, to use video most effectively, do not simply show the entire video in one sitting. Rather, scaffold the watching process carefully and have students view in an active, meaning-making mode. You might want to focus on particular scenes as your students read.

Performance Poetry
Analyzing Digital Video in Language Arts
GRADE LEVELS: 6–8

Objectives

- Students will be able to provide critical feedback.

- Students will be able to revise their own performance in response to feedback received from an audience.

National Council of Teachers of English/International Reading Association Standards (1996) Addressed

4. Students adjust their use of spoken, written, and visual language (e.g., conventions, style, vocabulary) to communicate effectively with different audiences for a variety of purposes

9. Students develop an understanding of and respect for diversity in language use, patterns, and dialects across cultures, ethnic groups, geographic regions, and social roles

11. Students participate as knowledgeable, reflective, creative and critical members of a variety of literacy communities

12. Students use spoken, written, and visual language to accomplish their own purposes (e.g., for learning, enjoyment, persuasion, and the exchange of information)

National Educational Technology Standards for Students (NETS·S) Addressed

1. **Creativity and Innovation**

    a. apply existing knowledge to generate new ideas, products, or processes

2. **Communication and Collaboration**

    a. interact, collaborate, and publish with peers, experts, or others employing a variety of digital environments and media

    b. communicate information and ideas effectively to multiple audiences using a variety of media and formats

    d. contribute to project teams to produce original works or solve problems

Technology/Materials Needed

- Video camera, or for live streaming, a webcam connected to a computer with a fast Internet connection

- Ustream.tv for streaming video of the live performance from one classroom to the other and for back-channel discussion during the performance. (Alternatively, you can record a performance for asynchronous viewing by the partner classroom, and they may use a free tool such as found at http://CoverItLive.com to support the back-channel discussion.)

- A free, online database tool such as found on http://creator.zoho.com for collecting open-ended responses

CONTENT

Reading and writing poetry is a component of the English curricula from elementary to high school. Students may study poetry as readers, as writers, and, as in this activity, as speakers/performers. Performance poetry tasks students not only with writing their own poems, but also with reading them aloud in a way that engages, motivates, and draws in an audience. Often linked to hip hop, slam poetry, and other spoken-word movements, performance poetry not only enables students to exercise writing skills but also moves them to develop reading fluency as they read, reread, and read again—all in an attempt to develop a compelling performance.

Technology enables you to distribute students' performances (through digital video or, in this case, streamed video) to audiences well outside of the classroom. For example, a class in a southeastern rural area may connect with students in an after-school program in urban California. Technology can also open up feedback possibilities for your students, inviting comments throughout a presentation through back-channel chat (real-time online conversation during the performance about the performance taking place). Further, reading and writing can become recursive, as students have the texts of their own performance for their own viewing, critique, and analysis and as artifacts prompting their own goal setting and improvement in subsequent performances.

TECHNOLOGY

The project may be undertaken in a technology-rich, highly involved manner or implemented using a fairly bare-bones approach. For example, one computer connected to a relatively fast Internet connection can be paired with a webcam to set up the classroom recording area. Student groups can broadcast their performances as part of a class structure with a variety of learning stations. There is no need for the entire class to watch as each student records or broadcasts a poem.

Handling streaming video is often challenging within a classroom context. On one hand, bandwith and connection speed is a factor in ensuring that the broadcast can be done. On the other, assuming that such a connection is in place, school policies differ tremendously regarding ways students appear (and are identified) in any online content. You can stream video using a nonidentifiable username and avoid revealing any student names. Tag and discuss performances by title of the poem rather than by student name.

If time-zone access is a problem, the performances can be viewed after being recorded, as opposed to being viewed live.

This project could be accomplished by exchanging files recorded in the classroom. However, audience participation and feedback may be limited. More importantly, students will not have an artifact of the performance integrating both the back-channel discussion and comments documented after the performance (database comments).

PEDAGOGY

Students are accustomed to reading and writing poetry in English class, yet few have the opportunity to add voice, movement, and performance to their work, putting a new spin on the question "Will you listen to my poem?"

Setup for the activity requires some preliminary work, depending on the activity's scope. Streaming student performances is only purposeful if there is an audience on the other end. So you will want to consider partnering with a teacher who will be as motivated to try this initiative as you are.

The driving factors here are the class objectives and goals. Connecting to an audience hinges on what skills students need to exercise. For example, you may want to focus on language play, point of view, and perspectives and, therefore, seek to partner with a class in a community providing students with different opportunities and experiences than those provided your own students. You can use a site such as http://globalschoolnet.org to search for such a classroom.

After your students share performances with the partner class, they can receive formal feedback through a database of prompts set up in an online database (using the free online tools at http://creator.zoho.com). The partner class can then stream its student performances, and your class can provide feedback.

> ### BACK-CHANNEL DISCUSSIONS
>
> Ustream.tv synchronous back-channel discussion must occur during the live stream. To support back-channel discussion when viewing a previously recorded performance, use free tools such as those available at www.CoverItLive.com.

Analysis is central to this project, as students focus on their own analysis of their written texts in developing a performance of the piece, analysis of the feedback received, analysis of the back-channel discussion during the performance, analysis of their peers' work, and so on. You will want to start by asking students to notice and articulate what they see when viewing the performance, to reflect and to set goals for future work given what they have seen, and to consider the ways feedback from others complicates or enriches their thinking.

At first, students may examine surface-level observations about eye contact, projection, or even inflection during the performance. Some might even critique camera angle or balance of the tripod. With some prompting, students will move from observing to listening.

At this stage, comments and feedback shift to examining the actual text presented by looking at literary elements (e.g., metaphor, tempo, voice), which can be amplified by the writer and which help each participant in the discussion with their own writing. We call this "listening as a writer." Analysis will also include the pairing of specific movements with lines of the text, sometimes in an attempt to "punctuate" the writing and at other times in an attempt to elicit emotion from the viewer/participant.

Analysis may reveal cultural differences as well, both in lived experiences in rural versus urban settings and in values of the ethnicities and communities within which each student participated. For example, a prompt modeled from Whitman's "I sing of America..." might challenge students to write their own "I hear... I see..." poetry. Poems (and their performance) can provide a specific, powerful lens into divergent perspectives and experiences.

Because Ustream.tv allows for recording and archiving of streamed broadcasts, and pairs easily with back-channel tools that record discussions, you and your students have access to their work over the course of a semester—or for as long a span of time as the project/work continues. This feature is important in opening up the opportunity for students to analyze their work over time, reflecting on their growth and development and the ways they have integrated the feedback received in earlier performances. In other words, the digital video created serves as an artifact of student work in a specific context and time. A collection of videos over time would provide the terms for a careful examination of how the analysis informed subsequent work, reflection, and goal setting—a powerful example of reflective practice for any teacher.

MORE IDEAS FOR ANALYZING DIGITAL VIDEO IN LANGUAGE ARTS

Analyze television commercials as a part of critical media literacy. Given that adolescents are viewed as the ideal consumer and target audience for most of the world's commercial advertising, critical media literacy should be addressed to some extent in any English language arts classroom. If you or your students doubt this at all, be sure to view any of the following:

- Jhally, S. (Producer/Director). (2000). *Killing us softly 3: Advertising's image of women with Jean Kilbourne* [Motion picture]. United States: The Media Education Foundation.

- Rushkoff, D. (Writer/Host). (2001). *Frontline: The merchants of cool* [Television series episode]. United States: PBS.

- Rushkoff, D. (Writer/Host). (2004). *Frontline: The persuaders* [Television series episode]. United States: PBS.

Each of these documentaries provides critical insights into ways advertisers are intentional, strategic, and controversial in their methods for getting the attention of and manipulating teenage consumers. You can have students view various clips from these documentaries and analyze them, but more importantly, you can then have students analyze various commercials as a part of a critical media literacy unit that draws on these documentaries and related resources. PBS not only has both of these *Frontline* episodes available online as streaming video clips, but they also have curriculum materials for teachers.

Analyze thematic comparisons. Film can provide opportunities to juxtapose themes in print texts with those in movies. In effect, films can help students better understand classic literary texts by providing a contemporary lens through which to analyze, compare, and comprehend similar themes. For example, when reading John Donne's "Meditation 17," in which the theme that no man is an island unto himself is explored, you might also have students analyze the clip from *It's a Wonderful Life*, in which Clarence the angel demonstrates for George Bailey just how different life in Bedford Falls would have been if he had never existed. Other possible text and film pairings for thematic analysis include the following:

- Shakespeare's *Romeo and Juliet* and the film version of *West Side Story*

- *The Odyssey* and *O Brother, Where Art Thou?*

- *The Diary of Anne Frank* and *Life Is Beautiful*

- Shakespeare's *King Lear* and Kurosawa's *Ran*

- *Cry, the Beloved Country* and *The Power of One*

Digital Book Trailers
Creating Digital Video in Language Arts
GRADE LEVELS: 4–12

Objectives

- Students will be able to compose using digital video, audio, and still images.

- Students will be able to promote a print text through the selection of key scenes or content.

National Council of Teachers of English/International Reading Association Standards (1996) Addressed

3. Students apply a wide range of strategies to comprehend, interpret, evaluate and appreciate texts. They draw on their prior experience, their interactions with other readers and writers, their knowledge of word meaning and of other texts, their word identification strategies, and their understanding of textual features (e.g., sound-letter correspondence, sentence structure, context, graphics).

8. Students use a variety of technological and information resources (e.g., libraries, databases, computer networks, video) to gather and synthesize information and to create and communicate knowledge

12. Students use spoken, written, and visual language to accomplish their own purposes (e.g., for learning, enjoyment, persuasion, and the exchange of information)

National Educational Technology Standards for Students (NETS·S) Addressed

1. **Creativity and Innovation**

   a. apply existing knowledge to generate new ideas, products, or processes

2. **Communication and Collaboration**

   a. interact, collaborate, and publish with peers, experts, or others employing a variety of digital environments and media

   b. communicate information and ideas effectively to multiple audiences using a variety of media and formats

   d. contribute to project teams to produce original works or solve problems

4. **Critical Thinking, Problem Solving, and Decision Making**

   b. plan and manage activities to develop a solution or complete a project

6. **Technology Operations and Concepts**

   a. understand and use technology systems

Technology/Materials Needed

- Access to still images and video clips, as well as music and other sound clips (any of which students may acquire themselves or download from the web)

- Digital video editing tools (such as iMovie, Movie Maker, or free web-based tools)

CONTENT

Often, the most effective uses of technology in the classroom are in direct response to challenging instructional "puzzles" emerging from traditional or familiar activities. For example, Web 2.0 technologies open up opportunities for an audience to view and provide feedback on student work. For this project, technology provides an answer to the instructional challenge created by independent reading tasks, often assigned in English classrooms but rarely evaluated. Further, these tasks also put a spotlight on the student readers in the classroom who are reading below level and for whom independent reading is ineffective without teacher scaffolds and support.

The book trailer project challenges students to play with the genre of the movie trailer, creating a short (2- to 3-minute) video that persuades viewers to read the text. Students must read and reread the text, then develop a storyboard of images evoked by the content of the book and write a script that advances the message within the trailer. Meaning in this project is a function of images paired with a narrated script, but it is also multiplicative, making the whole much greater than the sum of its parts. The final product should resemble a film, not a slide show presentation.

Distribution is a critical component of the work. This project could be completed offline through the use of school and local libraries (e.g., setting up a computer near the card catalog). Web 2.0 tools make sharing book trailers with a broader audience a simple task. The critical factor here is ensuring that students receive feedback on their work, ranging from specific comments (perhaps posted to a blog), to a clustermap linked to the class website or blog, to the hit counter on the bottom of a web page. Offline feedback can range from a book of entries kept near a screening computer in the library, to a count of the number of times the specific book has been checked out of the library after a user has viewed the related book trailer. Part of making this activity relevant to your students is ensuring an invested audience on the other end of the project.

PEDAGOGY

Students begin with reading. As useful as this activity is when linked to independent reading, anchoring those selections to a specific prompt can also yield useful results. For example, asking students to focus on a book they would recommend for "hooking" a reluctant reader levels the playing field. The focus becomes the appeal of a book rather than the reading level. Prompts need to consider both your instructional goals and the particular context in which you teach. You might even consider partnering your class with a class of younger reluctant readers and having your students target books for them.

After reading the selected text, students begin with a storyboard that visually maps out the material they envision playing on the "screen" during the trailer. (See Figure 4.3 for a sample page from a storyboard. For tips on storyboarding, see Chapter 7: "Creating Digital Video.") Running under the images are additional lines, sequencing narration with the images and layering in plans for sounds, effects, and motion. This work is all preplanning and drafting, but it pushes students back into the text repeatedly to generate the right content.

This work is done apart from the computer. Instead, your instructional talk should focus on the genre of the movie trailer, considering what is shown (and what isn't), how a "slice" of content represents the fuller text, how soundtrack functions to create mood, how print text functions when on the screen, and so on. Have students read sample movie trailers and then reread the independent reading texts. Then have them continue to plan and begin creating.

The next step of the work can occur largely outside of the classroom. Students need to locate the digital content (images, music, sounds) that follows the cues in the storyboard. Where students could use online image libraries for this work, they should be encouraged to create original images. Creating original images is as much a tool for teaching about copyright and fair use as it is a catalyst for students' visual composing.

In the classroom, have students work on revising their work, writing recursively by working back and forth between the image and the script (or text that might appear on the screen), or writing, revising, and editing as ideas arise through discussion and peer review.

After the script and storyboard are stable, invite your students to create their trailers in the computer lab (or with laptops if a cart is available). Keeping this step brief ensures that students maximize their time. Class instructional time needs to be focused on genre study, reading comprehension, and multimodal composing, not on bells and whistles layered on the trailer in extra lab time. One class period is likely more than enough time to produce a well-developed trailer, especially when the precomposing and preplanning were well conceived through the storyboard and script writing.

Where this work is driven by the pairing of good books and the power of self-expression, publishing the trailers through a public viewing is an effective means of supporting students' work as readers, as writers, and as reviewers who can provide critique and response when viewing work as a class. Having students show these during class is one option, but you can also explore posting them online for public viewing as well. Further, it is useful to examine different book trailers for the same text in order to examine multiple readings, various perspectives, multiple ways of representing meaning-making, and so on.

FIGURE 4.3. First page of a student storyboard for a book trailer about *The Andromeda Strain.*

MORE IDEAS FOR CREATING DIGITAL VIDEO IN LANGUAGE ARTS

Create proactive television commercials and public service announcements. Building on the previous idea associated with enhancing critical medial literacy, you could have students script, storyboard, and film their own proactive and ethically responsible television commercials for products they deem appropriate for their demographic. Similarly, they could also create public service announcements commenting on any ad campaigns they find particularly unethical or problematic.

Create digital video thematic explorations. Your students are probably all too familiar with identifying and defining vocabulary words, literary terms, and themes as a part of their literature studies. Why limit them to the dictionary? Instead, have your students work in small groups to brainstorm, write, storyboard, and film a representation of a given term or theme—a DV Sound Bite (Young, 2009). For example, if you were going to teach Orwell's *1984*, you might want to focus on the theme of conformity. In fact, you might have students create a video as a prereading activity to bridge into a particular thematic unit or piece of literature focused on a particular theme.

FIGURE 4.4. Front and back of DVD case students made for *The Andromeda Strain* video book trailer.

Then, you might have the groups create a second video after they have concluded all of the reading and related work for the unit that has informed their understanding of that particular theme. Afterwards, students can juxtapose the two videos to see if their unit work altered their understanding and portrayal of the particular theme. Regarding *1984*, chances are that students' videos conceptualizing conformity will change from a more benign representation prior to reading the novel to one that carefully considers the oppressive nature of Orwell's dystopian society.

Conclusion

THOUGH SEVERAL of the examples discussed in this chapter rely on newly emerging Web 2.0 and multimodal composition tools, at the core of the work are the opportunities such tools create for students to work as readers, writers, speakers, listeners, and thinkers. As much as some of these tasks can be done in different ways without technology or without the literacies new tools make possible, the right combination of instructional challenge/task and writing space/tool allows us to amplify our teaching and accomplish goals we couldn't previously manage.

Teachers do not necessarily need to know each new tool that emerges. Nor does every lesson or activity need to be deeply steeped in multimodal practices or new literacies in order to prepare students for the 21st-century workforce. Different teaching contexts will create different opportunities, some requiring us to go low-tech and trailing-edge. What matters is creating opportunities for students to use multiple means for communicating what they know and for communicating that knowledge within communities that can put that knowledge to work.

In doing so, we ratchet up the possibilities for engaging students, creating purposeful assignments, and challenging students to learn across multimodal texts using various tools that provide opportunities for exercising the ways they are multiply literate. We work to dissolve boundaries between inside and outside the classroom and help all students become literate in the dominant media of their generation.

More and more, digital video is becoming the dominant medium in which students engage—certainly out of school and increasingly in school as well. The activities described here offer only a small glimpse of the larger picture of possible applications for integrating digital video into English language arts instruction. However, they serve to illustrate how students can engage in the critical acts of watching, analyzing, and creating digital videos. These examples reflect a range of technologies, from simple tools to more complex ones, from free, online tools to commercial ones.

As you design your own activities with digital video, keep in mind the various options available to you and the ways in which you can maximize tools and resources to accomplish your pedagogical and content goals.

References

Coiro, J., Knobel, M., Lankshear, C., & Leu, D. (Eds.). *Handbook of research in new literacies*. Mahwah, NJ: Erlbaum.

Dalton, B., & Proctor, C. P. (2008). The changing landscape of text and comprehension in the age of new literacies. In J. Coiro, M. Knobel, C. Lankshear, & D. Leu (Eds.), *Handbook of research in new literacies* (pp. 297-324). Mahwah, NJ: Erlbaum.

National Council of Teachers of English/International Reading Association. (1996). *Standards for the English language arts.* Retrieved from www.ncte.org/standards

International Society for Technology in Education. (2007). *National educational technology standards for students* (2nd ed.). Eugene, OR: Author.

Lindfors, J. W. (1999). *Children's inquiry: Using language to make sense of the world.* New York, NY: Teachers College Press.

National Council of Teachers of English. (2008). *The NCTE definition of 21st century literacies.* Retrieved from www.ncte.org/positions/statements/21stcentdefinition

O'Brien, D. (2006). "Struggling" adolescents' engagement in multimediating: Countering the institutional construction of incompetence. In D. Alvermann, K. Hinchman, D. Moore, S. Phelps, & D. Waff (Eds.), *Reconceptualizing the literacies in adolescents' lives* (2nd ed., pp. 29-46). Mahwah, NJ: Erlbaum.

Partnership for 21st Century Skills. (2008). *21st century skills map: English.* Retrieved from www.21stcenturyskills.org/documents/21st_century_skills_english_map.pdf

Young, C. A. (2009, March). *Narrative and video in the English language arts classroom: Digital video and new literacies: Vignettes from the Field Symposium.* Paper presented at the annual meeting of the Society for Information Technology and Teacher Education, Charleston, SC.

CHAPTER 5

*Michael Searson, Curby Alexander,
and Dina Rosen*

digital video and
informal learning ■

turning the lens outside
the classroom

Students and New Media

NEW, OR "emergent," media—including blogs and wikis, video-sharing sites, online games, social network sites, iPods, and mobile phones—are playing a powerful role in the lives of many of today's youth outside of school. Students can post homemade videos on their Facebook or MySpace pages and expect feedback from peers included in their network. They also provide commentary to the videos posted on their friends' pages.

Students born in 1990 or later—known as *digital natives* (Prensky, 2001)—probably cannot remember a time when video could not be played on a computer. The first version of QuickTime emerged around this time, and the use of digital video has dramatically increased since then. The latest survey results from the Pew Internet and American Life project (Rainie, 2009) reported that approximately 40% of U.S. teens own a video camera, and more than 75% of them view videos on video-sharing websites. Furthermore, around 25% of American teens—slightly more than 5 million teenagers—have uploaded video to a video-sharing website. Presumably, most teens use video-sharing websites for entertainment and recreation, but there is evidence that in some cases students are creating videos independently for school projects.

A search using the term "school project" on YouTube will reveal dozens of videos created by students for school projects (Figure 5.1). These videos range from recordings of science experiments, to music videos about social issues, to remixes of historical events or classic films. The quality of these videos is also diverse, with some of them being well planned and of high quality, and others being rudimentary and impromptu.

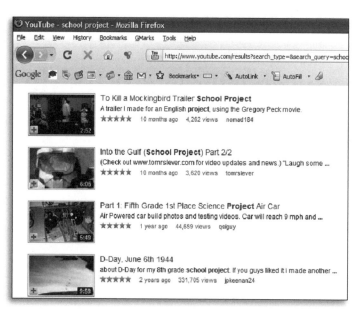

FIGURE 5.1. A selection of YouTube videos created by students for school projects.

Formal vs. Informal Learning Environments

ONE CHARACTERISTIC each of these school project videos has in common is that they have been viewed hundreds—sometimes thousands—of times and have received dozens of comments from viewers. This cycle of posting content and getting peer feedback is reminiscent of some classic education theories (such as those proposed by Piaget, Vygotsky, and Bandura), which argued that social interaction is a key mechanism in the process of learning and development. More contemporary theorists (e.g., Lave & Wenger, 1991; Rogoff, 1990) have said that learning occurs best (and naturally) in "socially mediated learning" environments, called "communities of practice." Wenger defined communities of practice as "groups of people who share a concern or a passion for something they do and learn how to do it better as they interact regularly" (Wenger, 2006). Thus, the viral social network developed in recent years over the creation and sharing of digital video can, itself, be characterized as a community of practice and may have important implications for student learning.

A number of educators maintain that informal learning (learning that takes place outside the formal classroom context) is often mediated within a social context. Informal learning can place a greater emphasis on social interactions and may lead to deeper learning. The National Science Foundation now funds grants for informal science education, designed specifically to support programs that use informal practices as tools to enhance learning of science, technology, engineering, and mathematics.

Communities of practice often support a collaborative approach to learning, recommended by key standards documents. For example, the recent revision of the National Educational Technology Standards for Students (International Society for Technology in Education, 2007) included a focus on communication and collaboration (Standard 2):

2. **Communication and Collaboration**
   Students use digital media and environments to communicate and work collaboratively, including at a distance, to support individual learning and contribute to the learning of others. Students:

   a. interact, collaborate, and publish with peers, experts, or others employing a variety of digital environments and media

   b. communicate information and ideas effectively to multiple audiences using a variety of media and formats

   c. develop cultural understanding and global awareness by engaging with learners of other cultures

   d. contribute to project teams to produce original works or solve problems

In its section titled Skills Framework, the Partnership for 21st Century Skills (2007) also addressed communication and collaboration, delineating the following skills:

Communicate Clearly

- Articulate thoughts and ideas effectively using oral, written and nonverbal communication skills in a variety of forms and contexts

- Listen effectively to decipher meaning, including knowledge, values, attitudes and intentions

- Use communication for a range of purposes (e.g., to inform, instruct, motivate and persuade)

- Utilize multiple media and technologies, and know how to judge their effectiveness a priori as well as assess their impact

- Communicate effectively in diverse environments (including multi-lingual)

Collaborate with Others

- Demonstrate ability to work effectively and respectfully with diverse teams

- Exercise flexibility and willingness to be helpful in making necessary compromises to accomplish a common goal

- Assume shared responsibility for collaborative work, and value the individual contributions made by each team member

These standards notably reflect the 21st-century environment in which today's students thrive and the type of workforce they can expect to enter.

Unfortunately, communities of practice are difficult to implement and sustain in current K–12 classroom settings (formal learning environments). Communities of practice are not completely foreign to K–12 schools, however. In fact, they have thrived for many years in informal learning environments taking the form of competitive teams, clubs, and after-school programs. Students are drawn to these groups based on personal interests and goals, and in many cases the participants learn as much from each other as they do from the coach or sponsor. Table 5.1 presents a comparison of formal and informal learning environments.

There are a variety of characteristics that differentiate informal learning environments from their formal counterparts, and the settings in which the learning takes place can be quite diverse as well. In some cases, the informal learning is manifested as a search for videos of interest using the World Wide Web. In other instances, the informal learning environment is planned by a teacher but takes place outside the school campus and at a time when school is not in session. In the section that follows are several examples of the various roles digital video plays in a broad spectrum of informal learning environments.

TABLE 5.1. Comparison of Formal and Informal Learning Environments

FORMAL LEARNING ENVIRONMENTS	INFORMAL LEARNING ENVIRONMENTS
Constrained by time, both in terms of allocated time and pacing Schools allow teachers a predetermined amount of time to address the required topics each day. The average school day is 7 hours, and a middle level or secondary teacher sees each student for approximately an hour each day. Teachers must meticulously plan their instruction at the beginning of each school year to ensure that each topic is covered before the end-of-year assessment. Elementary teachers have more flexibility in how they allocate time, but they still must carefully pace their instruction so that each topic is covered before the students are tested.	**May have constraints on allocated time, but not on pacing** Competitive teams, clubs, or after-school programs are usually given a specific amount of time in which to meet with students, but there is typically more freedom in what topics are addressed and how time is used.
Teachers and students are accountable to the learning standards, which may or may not be of personal interest K–12 schools are accountable to state and district content-area learning standards that must be covered in a finite amount of time. Although some students will demonstrate genuine engagement with the subject matter addressed by their teachers, most of them will do the required work in order to sustain acceptable grades, maintain their eligibility for extracurricular activities, or avoid negative consequences from parents and teachers.	**Opportunity to pursue learning of subject matter of personal interest** Informal learning environments are typically student centered and allow students to work toward group or individual goals that interest them personally. In fact, this personal interest is what normally draws students to join such groups.
Student participation is mandated In a formal learning environment, participation is not typically optional. Many teachers assign a point value to class participation as a way to keep students engaged. Furthermore, students are required to attend school, either by state laws or by their parents.	**Student participation is voluntary** Most students join teams and clubs by their own choice. Student who lose interest in the club for some reason are not required to continue participating.
Knowledge expression is typically convergent (guiding students toward common understanding) The objective for much of the instruction in formal learning environments is to make sure students can recall the answers to the assignments given to them by teachers.	**Knowledge expression can be divergent (students respond to the subject in different ways, which leads to diverse understandings)** Because learning standards are not the focus of informal learning environments, students may leave shared experiences, such as a trip to a museum, with very different interpretations and impressions.

Digital Video as an Informal Learning Resource

FOR DECADES people have watched video or movies in groups, whether at home or in theaters. However, when today's youth watch digital videos, it is almost always against the backdrop of a broader socially mediated network. They also understand how to use that network as a valuable resource.

Video-sharing websites host instructional videos ranging from class lectures, to screen-casts of commonly used software applications, to physical demonstrations. These videos are posted by people with a personal interest in some particular subject matter, and they are accessed by people with a similar interest and a desire to learn something new. For example, one of the most highly viewed YouTube videos in past years was that of a popular hip-hop and dance artist, in which he demonstrated step-by-step how to do his signature dance. The video is four minutes long and to date has been viewed over 41 million times! Sixty-seven thousand of those viewers have rated the video (on a 5-star scale), more than 52,000 people have left a text comment, and nearly 400 viewers have created their own video in response to this one. A more detailed analysis of this video reveals not only *who* is watching, but *how* they are watching the video. Programmers on the YouTube team have been able to measure at which point viewers quit watching the video, and they have determined that many viewers watch the video until a certain dance step, then rewatch that dance step multiple times by dragging the scrub bar backward. This scenario, though not academic in nature, serves as an example for how teens are using web-based video to learn things that are of personal interest to them.

Media-Enhanced Field Trips

OVER THE summer, a group of 31 students and three sponsors participated in a two-week camp in which they traveled to eight historic sites in the mid-Atlantic area, such as Gettysburg and Harper's Ferry (Figure 5.2). The students ranged in age from 14 to 17, and they came from five different states. Participants were placed in groups of two to three students, and each group was given a video camera, digital still camera, and digital audio recorder. Each group's objective was to create a short documentary film illustrating the concept of leadership, using the key figures from each of the historic sites as examples.

Before the students began filming, they read background materials for each of the sites they would be visiting. This activity helped them develop an overall theme for their movie as well as plan out the exact monuments and locations they wanted to capture for their film. Knowing what they were looking for ahead of time helped the students use their time more efficiently while at the sites. They knew that time lost at the sites was time lost forever, because there was no time to go back and reshoot footage.

FIGURE 5.2. A student captures video of his classmates touring a Revolutionary War-era cemetery during a media-enhanced field trip to Harper's Ferry, West Virginia.

Students also had the opportunity to practice capturing footage from a variety of perspectives and with different amounts of lighting. They would take turns with the camera capturing images of the same objects from different angles, then compare those images and video clips to evaluate which would be most effective for different parts of their movie. Again, students could maximize their time while on location and create the best movie possible using the time they were given.

Having a plan for which footage the students wanted to capture also inspired spontaneous ideas once they were on location. For example, while in Harper's Ferry, one of the groups saw some girls in traditional costumes singing songs from the early 1800s. The group member with the digital audio recorder quickly ran over to capture a few of their songs, which became part of the background music for their movie. Other groups captured video and audio of tour guides, storytellers, and historical reenactors, which the groups were not expecting to see but knew would enhance their movies.

Once the students were back at the school, they began working on their movies. In order to manage the workflow of these projects, the students were given specific directions about which tasks had to be completed and in which order. For example, the students were told to load all of their media onto the computers, using folders to separate images, video, and audio. They then engaged in the task of editing their movie down to four minutes or less. One of the adult sponsors was required to monitor their progress before they were allowed to proceed to the next step in the process.

The groups finally finished their movies, complete with sound and special effects, and a local filmmaker was brought in to speak to the group and view the movies. The students were able to share what they had learned not only about each period in history, but also about leadership and the process of making movies. The movies were all burned onto a DVD for the students to take with them, and they were posted to the host organization's website as a way to attract future participants.

Extended Educational Travel

ON A TRIP even further from home, a group of educators and college students went to Costa Rica on an educational tour designed to blend emergent media tools with explorations of global education. These media tools allowed participants to reflect on their travels and experiences and communicate directly with friends and family members back home (and across the world).

Travelers used an assortment of technology they carried around with them in backpacks (including a wireless laptop, a voice recorder, a digital camera, and a headset with microphone). Many travelers updated their blogs every other day, enhancing their posts with photos, digital stories, and podcasts. Through the comments feature, friends and family members could easily respond to posts and become part of the adventure.

On an educational tour to Paris, a college business student designed an exemplary blog (see http://chantefernandez-travelearnparis2007.blogspot.com). Her blog includes wonderful design elements, and her writing reflects the richness of her experience and how she was able to integrate her travels into a meaningful learning event. Arguably, her blog demonstrates deep reflection that goes well beyond anything that could be captured by a more traditional approach of snapping a series of photos and then sharing them with friends and family once she returned home.

Another student's work while on an educational tour in Peru led to the development of a rich website, which among other things provides WebQuest-type lesson plans. Her Anything But Square Design website can be viewed at www.anythingbutsquaredesign. com.

A classroom teacher on the same Peru trip not only used her blog, iChat, and Skype to communicate with her students back home in California, but extended rich work in the exploration of water quality in many ways, even after the trip's conclusion. (See Figure 5.3 and http://web.mac.com/elainewrenn/Site/Welcome.html.)

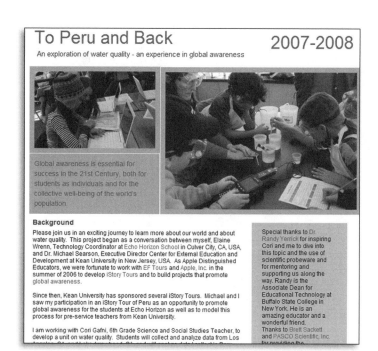

FIGURE 5.3. Screenshot of Elaine Wrenn's blog about her educational trip to Peru.

Using a GPS device, some travelers have engaged in geocaching, a contemporary form of treasure hunting. (See www.geocaching.com.) Increasingly, geocaching activities are being integrated into educational experiences, from social studies to geology to library sciences (see, for example, Lewis & McLelland, 2007; White-Taylor & Donellon, 2008; Wright, Inman, & Wilson, 2008).

By combining Google Earth and Keyhole Markup Language (KML), usually zipped as KMZ files, with geocaching, students can make rich videos that reflect geocaching adventures. The Google Earth Blog (www.gearthblog.com/reference.html) provides many resources for those who wish to explore the integration of these tools. In addition to enhancing 21st-century literacies, the application of digital media and web tools to international travel experiences provides a level of engagement and opportunity for reflection that can only deepen global education.

Connecting with the Local Community

STUDENT FACILITY with digital media tools also served as a catalyst for a unique project involving a public college, a Public Broadcasting Service (PBS) affiliate, and several high schools. Digital media tools were employed to supplement the broadcast of the Ken Burns documentary *The War* during the 2007-08 academic year. Project participants were provided with wireless laptops, digital voice recorders, digital cameras, and camcorders.

FIGURE 5.4. Using a voice-recorder-equipped iPod, a high school student interviews New Jersey Governor Jon Corzine as part of a school project on WWII. Digital story-telling techniques were later employed to make a video of the project.

The students and teachers involved in the project were asked to use these digital media tools to tell community stories related to World War II, ranging from interviews with veterans, including grandparents and local politicians, to little-known community WWII stories.

Student and teacher engagement was high throughout the duration of this project. Community fascination with the work of these students and teachers was so high that participants were given unusual access to local and statewide leaders (including the current and two former New Jersey governors, Figure 5.4). One team was even allowed to interview key figures involved in the making of the Burns documentary.

The multimedia projects created in this initiative were broadcast to viewers through a number of delivery systems, from podcasts to YouTube videos to local cable TV broadcasts. An estimated 35,000 people viewed the resulting projects (including large numbers of cable television viewers). As some of the work is now available through iTunes U, these numbers will likely grow.

Once the project was completed, faculty and staff began to consider how these tools and techniques could be imported into other curriculum projects. One teacher used the same tools to engage students in a water quality study of a local pond. She also podcast that work. The incentive to replicate highly visible and successful projects cannot be underes-timated. Additionally, when these successful digital media projects featuring community and political leaders receive positive public scrutiny, future integration of digital media projects into the curriculum is greatly enhanced and usually received with enthusiasm.

These few rich examples of learners engaged in informal learning through digital media outside traditional classroom settings encourage us to consider more seriously how digital media connect with the goals of sound classroom pedagogy: engaging with rich content, working in collaborative environments, demonstrating competency when researching a topic, and exploring 21st-century literacies.

You can empower students to become even more proficient in activities that naturally interest them. Organic experiences derived from informal learning opportunities can be channeled into more goal-oriented activities. When students are creating digital videos, their normally spontaneous tendencies can be supplemented by thorough planning (such as storyboarding) that will result in less editing after the initial shooting and a more focused production. Purpose, message, meaning, and audience can all be considered at the front end of a project.

Structuring Informal Learning Environments

WHEN PLANNING an informal learning experience using digital video, such as an after-school or summer program, there are a few principles that should be followed. Foremost, the emphasis in these groups should be on student interest, not on learning standards. There may be opportunities to introduce or review academic topics, but that should not be the focus of the program. If students see an advertisement for an after-school video club, they will attend expecting to learn how to make videos.

Find out what students want to learn about filmmaking and allow them to pursue those interests. Classroom projects using digital video typically do not allow enough time for students to experiment with many of the techniques they have seen used in the movies they watch. Ask students what movies they like to watch or what characteristics they find interesting in their favorite movies. There may even be time to watch clips from movies that illustrate these techniques. If the students are old enough, they can fill out a short survey or questionnaire about what they hope to learn from participating in the activity.

Students in the enhanced field trip example were given the opportunity to explore different angles, lighting, and perspectives. They were given several brief challenges to see who could come up with the most creative angle or perspective. Participants spread out over a large area of grass could be seen on their bellies, sitting on each other's shoulders, and even hanging upside down from trees. They learned that every single aspect of a movie must be carefully planned out, and that changing even one angle can alter the movie's interpretation.

Video is becoming synonymous with live-action footage captured with a camcorder, but there are other forms of filmmaking that students may find engaging. Informal learning environments provide a good opportunity to introduce alternative filmmaking techniques, such as stop-motion animation and clay animation. These forms of filmmaking create opportunities to introduce other skills, such as how to use various computer software programs, photography, and sculpture.

Provide general themes and allow students freedom to be creative within those themes. This format has traditionally been used by National History Day, where students are given a general theme and have the freedom to explore any facet of history they find of personal interest. For example, the theme for National History Day during the 2008–2009 school year was The Individual in History: Actions and Legacies. Variations on this theme included documentaries about individuals ranging from Clara Lemlich to Ben Kuroki to Rachel Carson. Themes help provide structure to a film project, yet they allow enough freedom for personal expression.

When possible, shoot video footage at various locations, such as historic sites, local attractions, and authentic settings. Students may also enjoy capturing footage in various locations at their school. For instance, a group of third grade students recently wrote a story about a day their teacher was missing. They physically went to the locations in their story (such as the office, janitor's closet, and gymnasium) to shoot the scenes of their story. Had this project been done in a formal classroom environment, the students would likely have disturbed other classes and would have taken time away from other subjects. While on field trips, teachers are preoccupied with student behavior and making sure they all get on the bus, making it difficult to use those opportunities for capturing video. Informal learning environments typically have fewer students and allow teachers to work more closely with students.

Allow time for students to explore postproduction techniques, such as sound, visuals, and special effects. This very well may be the reason students chose to participate in the first place. If not told otherwise, students will immediately begin adding special effects to their movies before editing the content. Students growing up during this time in history have probably viewed thousands of movies in their lifetimes, and they are eager to reproduce some of the effects they have seen created in their favorite films. As an example, during the media-enhanced field trip, two boys asked one of the sponsors if he knew how to create the "Matrix effect" using iMovie. After the students had reached the required benchmarks, the instructor showed them how to replicate the desired effect in their own movie. This, in turn, led other students to want to learn other special effects techniques, some of which the instructor did not know how to create. Because the schedule was somewhat flexible, the students were able to explore iMovie and help each other fine-tune their movies with sound effects and video filters. Opportunities like these can dramatically increase students' engagement in the filmmaking process.

Teachers and sponsors should seek out opportunities for students to showcase and improve their work. There are currently several ongoing contests involving film and video:

- Best Fest America (www.bestfestsandiego.com)

- Studentfilms.com (www.studentfilms.com)

- Studentfilmakers.com: lists regional and national short-film competitions (www.studentfilmmakers.com/classifieds/view.php?cat=46)

- YouTube Contests (www.youtube.com/contests_main)

Teachers and New Media

STUDENTS ARE not the only ones who can benefit from the abundance of web-based media in today's society. Curriculum development and planning can be enhanced through appropriate use of digital video. You can find many videos to help you plan a lesson or unit. For example, a language arts teacher interested in using literature circles could view a group of teachers working together to plan a literature circle (search on "literature circles" at http://teachertube.com). You can even find valuable resources about the topic of digital video itself. To learn more about video podcasting, for example, you can go to the Common Craft website (www.commoncraft.com/podcasting) and view a short movie on the subject.

Conclusion

ALTHOUGH YOU may face many barriers (such as limited bandwidth, outdated equipment, restricted Internet access, and Internet safety issues) in trying to integrate emergent media and digital video into your curriculum, we encourage you to continue your commitment to providing the best education possible to your students. Such a commitment to today's youth will prepare students to be active learners equipped to fully participate as citizens in the 21st century.

References

International Society for Technology in Education (ISTE). (2007). *National educational technology standards and performance indicators for students.* Retrieved from www.iste.org/Content/NavigationMenu/NETS/ForStudents/2007Standards/NETS_for_Students_2007_Standards.pdf

Lave, J., & Wenger, E. (1991). *Situated learning: Legitimate peripheral participation.* Cambridge, UK: University of Cambridge.

Lewis, G. B., & McLelland, C. V. (2007). *EarthCaching—An educator's guide.* Retrieved from www.geosociety.org/earthcache/WebBook/EarthCaching_EducatorsGuide.pdf

Partnership for 21st Century Learning Skills. (2007). *Framework for 21st century learning: Communication and collaboration.* Retrieved from www.21stcenturyskills.org/index.php?option=com_content&task=view&id=261&Itemid=120

Prensky, M. (2001, October). Digital natives, digital immigrants. *On the Horizon, 9* (5).

Rainie, L. (2009, January). *Teens and the Internet.* Presentation at the Consumer Electronics Show—Kids@Play Summit [PowerPoint slides]. Retrieved from www.pewInternet.org/~/media//Files/Presentations/2009/2009%20-%201.9.09%20-%20Teens%20and%20the%20internet-%20CES.ppt.ppt

Rogoff, B. (1990). *Apprenticeship in thinking: Cognitive development in social context.* New York, NY: Oxford University Press.

Wenger, E. (2006, June). Communities of practice: A brief introduction. Retrieved from www.ewenger.com/theory

White-Taylor, J., & Donellon, P. (2008). Geocaching in education. In K. McFerrin et al. (Eds.), *Proceedings of Society for Information Technology and Teacher Education International Conference 2008* (pp. 5340–5342). Chesapeake, VA: Association for the Advancement of Computers in Education.

Wright, V. H., Inman, C. T., & Wilson, E. K. (2008). Get up, get out with geocaching: Engaging technology for the social studies classroom [Electronic version]. *Social Studies Research and Practice, 3*(3). Retrieved from http://socstrp.org/issues/PDF/3.3.6.pdf

PART 2

digital video
technology

CHAPTER 6

Bernard Robin and
Daniel Tillman

acquiring digital video

DURING THE past several decades, an almost complete transformation has taken place in the way information is created, shared, and used. The use of traditional analog tools such as typewriters, phonograph records, films, and standard televisions has declined as they have been replaced by their digital counterparts: computers, compact discs and MP3 files, digital videos, and high-definition broadcasts. Most people consider this new generation of digital tools to be more precise, better sounding, clearer looking, and in general, superior in overall quality and convenience. Certainly, the ability to easily, quickly, and inexpensively record, edit, and share digital moving images has been revolutionary for amateur videographers of all ages.

Whereas editing and sharing video is addressed in subsequent chapters, this chapter provides an overview of the various ways in which digital video can be acquired:

- Playing digital video on a computer

- Downloading video from the web

- Capturing video from your computer screen

- Embedding YouTube videos on your web page

- Digitizing video from VHS tapes

- Capturing video from broadcast, cable, or satellite TV

- Extracting video from DVDs

- Shooting your own video with a digital video camcorder

The chapter also includes links to a website with some tutorial-style instructions for various methods of acquiring video and sample videos demonstrating how these techniques can be used to create educational multimedia projects.

COPYRIGHT

Use of copyrighted matrial is covered in Appendix B, A Few Words about Copyright and Educational Use.

Playing Digital Video Clips on a Computer

TO VIEW any digital video on a computer, video-playing software is required. Sometimes, the video player is embedded in a web page, such as on YouTube or on some broadcast network websites with past episodes of television shows. Otherwise, you will need a separate software program.

Windows Media Player from Microsoft and Apple's QuickTime player are commonly found on modern desktop and laptop PCs and Macintosh computers, respectively, and new versions with added features are frequently released and easily downloaded and installed.

FLV players, for viewing clips in the more recent Flash video format, are available for Windows and Mac and can be downloaded for free from CNET at www.cnet.com/topic-software/flv-player.html.

Just as digital images can be saved in different file formats such as JPEG, GIF, BMP, and PICT, digital video can be saved in a variety of file formats as well. Common digital video file formats are listed in Table 6.1, and some of the most popular free video player applications are listed in Table 6.2.

TABLE 6.1. Digital Video File Formats

FILE FORMAT	EXTENSION	CHARACTERISTICS
WINDOWS VIDEO	.avi	Older video format for PCs, good quality, large file size
WINDOWS MEDIA VIDEO	.wmv .asf	More recent video format for PCs, significantly better compression, good quality, smaller files
QUICKTIME	.mov .qt (Mac)	Default video format for Macintosh computers, good quality, large files, should play on both PCs and Macs
MPEG	.mpg .mpeg (Mac)	Versatile cross-platform ability, good compression, good quality, moderate file size
REAL VIDEO	.rm	Popular streaming audio and video format designed to play over the Internet on PCs and Macs, but not usually to be downloaded
FLASH VIDEO	.flv .swf	More recent video format popular on many websites (YouTube, Google Videos), designed to play over the Internet on PCs and Macs, but sometimes can be downloaded, too

TABLE 6.2. Examples of Free Digital Video Players

PLAYERS	OPERATING SYSTEM	FILE FORMATS SUPPORTED
WINDOWS MEDIA PLAYER	Windows	.avi, .wmv, .mpg, .mov, .mp4, .flv
QUICKTIME PLAYER	Mac and Windows	.mov, .qt, .mp4
VLC	Mac and Windows	.avi, .wmv, .mpg, .mov, .mp4, .flv
ALSHOW	Windows	.avi, .wmv, .mpg, .mov, .mp4, .flv
REALPLAYER	Mac and Windows	.rm, .avi, .wmv, .mpg, .mov, .mp4, .flv
FLV PLAYER	Mac and Windows	.flv, .swf

Downloading Video from the Web

THE WEB is a wonderful repository of video clips that span numerous content areas and time periods, but for a variety of reasons, you may want to download videos to your computer rather than watching them online. For instance, you may want to play a video

NEW MEDIA LITERACIES

By Michael Searson and Dina Rosen

Taking advantage of new and emergent media requires a number of new skills from both students and teachers. Here are two important skills for finding and critically selecting digital videos.

EFFECTIVE SEARCHING FOR DIGITAL VIDEOS ON THE WEB

The most common approach to searching for a digital video is "Googling" a title or topic or searching on the YouTube site. However, for students in schools, there are more effective (and safer) ways to conduct high-quality and educationally relevant searches. Most schools impose some type of filter on the Internet to prevent access to the most objectionable videos, but many videos can still be accessed that are inappropriate for school use.

■ Tools such as Google's "custom search" (see www.google.com/cse) can be used to develop targeted search engines relevant to the work at hand. For example, at http://google.com/coop/cse?cx=005924364887099665360%3Avbxf-mzrv4i, you will find a search engine that was created to "nurture girls' interest in science, technology, engineering, and math (STEM)." Visit that site, enter the term "STEM video," and see what you find.

■ By limiting your search to appropriate domains, you are more likely to find educationally relevant videos. For instance, by beginning your search with the phrase:

inurl:k12

and then adding the topic to be searched in quotation marks, you will limit your search to K–12 sites. For example, compare a search on:

barack obama video

to a search on:

inurl:k12 "barack obama video"

You will see, among other characteristics, that the "inurl:k12" search yields no commercial sites and locates a number of school-generated projects within the K–12 domain.

PURPOSEFULLY AND CRITICALLY SELECTING VIDEO FROM SOCIAL-SHARING SITES

In an age of abundant video available to (and often created by) today's youth, the ability to select videos critically from various networks becomes increasingly important. On the one hand, ratings tools give viewers a sense of how a video is regarded in the social network where it resides. For example, the YouTube site includes a five-star viewer rating system, viewer comments (available both in text and video), information about the video's author, and links to other videos the author may have posted.

Of course, the evaluation of videos within a social network is determined by those who frequent the network. For example, the hate-speech website http://martinlutherking.org is accompanied by a heavily subscribed-to forum filled with distorted, inaccurate, and racist statements about Dr. King. Discussing with students the nature of the social networks within which digital videos are posted can be powerful teachable moments.

offline or outside its web context. Or you may want to extract a short clip, remix the sequence of a video, or combine (or "mashup") multiple videos.

You probably already know how to download (or save) still images from websites, but downloading video from the web can be a bit more complicated. Not all digital video files found on the web are designed to be downloaded. Many are "streamed," which allows the video to be delivered to your computer gradually so it can begin playing more quickly; that is, you do not need to wait for the entire clip to be downloaded before playing. The disadvantage of this process is that many streamed video files cannot be easily saved for later viewing, nor can they be transferred from one computer to another. The files are only temporarily stored on your computer and disappear once they have been watched.

Some video repository sites, such as TeacherTube and the SITE Screening Room, provide their own video downloader. The YouTube website (www.youtube.com), which is one of the most popular web resources for finding and viewing video clips, does not. The following section describes a variety of ways to transfer video from the web to your hard drive.

Saving Video to Your Hard Drive

VIDEOS THAT open in a video player on your computer, such as Windows Media Player (Figure 6.1), sometimes may be saved to your computer. An easy way to find out if you can download the video is go to the player's File menu and see whether the Save or Save As option is displayed. If it is, you may be able to easily save the video clip for later use. The Save option is not always available, often because the owner of the video prefers that it not be downloadable. (Note that not all video players include a Save option; the free Apple QuickTime Player does not, for example, whereas the Pro version does.)

FIGURE 6.1. The Save As option in Windows Media Player is located under the program's File menu.

Some recent versions of popular video players such as RealPlayer include an option for downloading video clips, including Flash-based videos and some streamed videos, from the web. The free player from www.real.com comes with both a web browser button and a mouse-over feature that allows users to download video clips directly from web pages.

Capturing Video from Your Computer Screen

IF YOU cannot easily download a video from the web, another option is to use screen capture software. These applications allow you to record anything on your computer screen (or any portion of your screen), including cursor movements. Many screen capture programs also allow you to record audio that is playing or to add your own audio narrations to the captured video (using a microphone).

Not only can you use these programs to capture video from the web, but you can also create your own instructional videos, or "screencasts," for any computer-based activity. Camtasia Studio for Windows, by TechSmith, and Adobe Captivate for Windows are both fairly expensive programs, but they include numerous features not found on other screen-recording programs—the most valuable of which is the capability to edit the video and audio captured with the respective programs. Neither Camtasia Studio or Adobe Captivate are currently available for the Macintosh operating system.

Snapz Pro X (Figure 6.2) is available for Mac users. It includes fewer features than Camtasia or Captivate, but SnapZ Pro is considerably less expensive and is a popular alternative for Mac users interested in creating screencasts. A number of free programs are available as well (see Table 6.3), although they generally do not include editing capability. To edit video captured with these programs, you would need to use separate video editing software.

More information about creating educational screencasts can be found in Chapter 7: "Creating Digital Video."

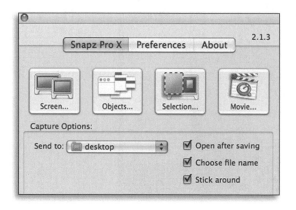

FIGURE 6.2. Screen capture options in Snapz Pro X for Macintosh computers.

TABLE 6.3. Free Screen Capture Programs

PROGRAM	OPERATING SYSTEM	DOWNLOAD LINK
AUTOSCREEN RECORDER	Windows	www.wisdom-soft.com/downloads/downloadfiles.htm
CAMSTUDIO	Windows	www.download.com/CamStudio/3000-13633_4-10067101.html
FREESCREENCAST.COM	Windows	http://freescreencast.com/pages/download
JING PROJECT	Mac and Windows	www.jingproject.com
SCREENTOASTER	Mac and Windows	www.screentoaster.com
WINK	Windows	www.debugmode.com/wink/download.php

Using Conversion Software

ANOTHER METHOD for capturing YouTube videos is to use the free web-based tool Media Converter (found at www.mediaconverter.org). This tool requires you to copy the URL of the video you wish to save (see Figure 6.3) and paste it into the Converter. Then, you select a video format in which to save the downloaded clip (Figure 6.4). YouTube uses the FLV Flash video format, which is common for videos that are streamed or played using a web-based video player. Other popular video formats, such as the QuickTime MOV format, may be a good choice because videos in this format usually play well on both PCs and Macintosh computers.

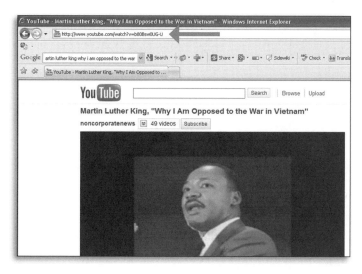

FIGURE 6.3. Screenshot showing selection of a direct URL to a YouTube video.

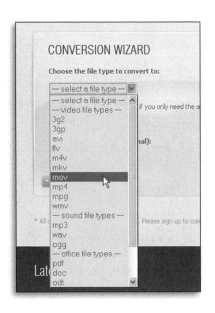

FIGURE 6.4. File type menu in Media Converter.

Embedding YouTube Videos in Your Web Page

YOU MAY prefer to embed YouTube videos in your own web page or in a blog or wiki for online viewing without the distracting comments and related video links included on the YouTube site. You may also find value in collecting multiple videos in one spot or providing opportunities for conversations around specific videos that are open only to your students (see more in Chapter 8: "Communicating with Digital Video").

The process for embedding YouTube videos is simple and straightforward, although video creators may disable the embed feature. If the embed feature is enabled, copy the HTML snippet found on the YouTube page for the video. Figure 6.5 shows an example of what the HTML snippet looks like.

FIGURES 6.5. Detail of a YouTube page showing the embed code for the video.

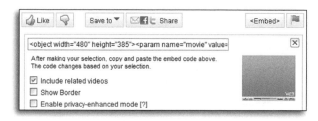

FIGURE 6.6. When you click on the embed code to the right of the YouTube video, a box like this one appears. By default, the "Include related videos" box is checked. We recommend unchecking this box before copying the embed code.

You may also want to uncheck the box that allows other "related" videos to be suggested at the end of the video you're embedding (Figure 6.6). Sometimes the videos that are suggested are not appropriate for students to see.

MORE ABOUT THE YOUTUBE SITE

By Lynn Bell

YouTube videos have raised social awareness, advanced political careers, and expressed countless teens' individuality. YouTube's value today is incalculable, and many students regularly view and upload videos on the site from their home computers. Despite its many positive uses, however, classroom use of the site may require some restrictions.

If you have spent any time on YouTube, you probably have noticed that even when viewing a preselected video on the site, you will encounter comments (sometimes unkind ones), a list of related videos (sometimes with vulgar titles), and advertising. Extracting videos or embedding them in your own website allows you to take advantage of the educational clips while avoiding the distractions.

You should check your school or district policy before sending your students to YouTube to search for videos. Besides the cruel and abusive comments that can be found with some videos, the content of the videos vary widely, from how-tos; laughing babies; and goofy songs to racist rants; dangerous, irresponsible behavior; and sexually provocative acts. YouTube provides flagging tools so that users can advise them of videos that violate site policies, but keeping up with hundreds of thousands of new videos being uploaded every day is not easy.

Your students will definitely benefit from discussions about focusing on the best YouTube has to offer and avoiding the worst.

Capturing Video from Offline Media

IN ADDITION to the enormous amount of digital video available on the Internet, there is an additional, endless supply of video available offline, in such formats as VHS tapes, television, and DVDs.

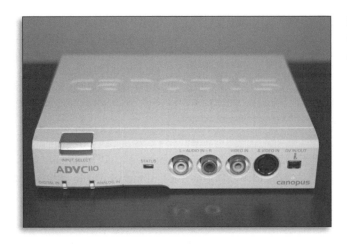

FIGURE 6.7. One type of VHS video digitizer is the Canopus ADVC110 Video Digitizer.

VHS TAPES

Even though VHS tapes are gradually being replaced by DVDs and other digital video technologies, large numbers of them still exist in households, schools, and libraries throughout the world. Some of these VHS tapes contain video segments with educational value. Transferring VHS video to digital format requires specialized hardware and software. Many different devices and software programs are available that can be used together to extract and preserve video stored on VHS tapes.

Pinnacle creates several easy-to-use and affordable packages. An example is their Dazzle Video Creator, which retails for $90 and allows you to connect an analog camcorder, VHS player, or DVD player through S-video or RCA cables to a capture device that interfaces with their video editing software (provided). They make a similar package for Apple computers, called Pinnacle Video Capture for Mac, for $100. They also have the Dazzle DVD Recorder, for $50, which digitizes from a VHS player directly to a DVD burner. Another company that manufactures analog video digitizers is Canopus, which makes the entry-level ADVC55 and ADVC110 (Figure 6.7).

The video digitizer is connected to a VCR or analog camcorder, from which it will receive the analog video signal, and then to a computer, which will be used to view the video and complete the digital conversion process. With some products, including those created by Pinnacle, all of the required software for digitizing analog video is included. With products such as those created by Canopus, a separate software program that can capture the digital signal is usually needed (unless the signal is being sent directly to a recording device such as a stand-alone DVD burner). Most commercially available video editing software packages, for example, Adobe Premiere Elements 3 or

USING VHS

More information on digitizing video clips from VHS tapes and a sample digital video project using such clips may be found online at http://site.aace.org/video/books/teaching/acquire/video2.htm.

higher, work with video digitizers. Free applications such as Windows Movie Maker and iMovie (included with the Apple operating system) also have video capture options available, albeit with fewer editing features.

BROADCAST, CABLE, OR SATELLITE TV

Educationally valuable video clips may also be acquired from broadcast, cable, or satellite television. Capturing television broadcasts requires both a hardware and software solution. Hardware devices, including the following popular models, are sold by many different manufacturers: the Pinnacle PCTV HD TV Tuner, Autumn Wave's OnAir Creator and HDTV-GT Receiver, the Leadtek Winfast TV2000 XP Expert, the MSI Theatre 650PRO TV Tuner, the Diamond Multimedia TV Wonder HD 650 PCI-Express X1 TV Tuner, and the Hauppauge WinTV-HVR 1600 TV Tuner. Prices range from slightly less than $70 to more than $200, depending on the level of sophistication of the hardware and included software (Figure 6.8). The more expensive packages have features designed for enhancing recreational use of the equipment that are generally gratuitous for educational purposes.

USING CABLE TV

More information on capturing video clips from cable television and a sample digital video project using such clips may be found online at http://site.aace.org/video/ books/teaching/acquire/ video3.htm.

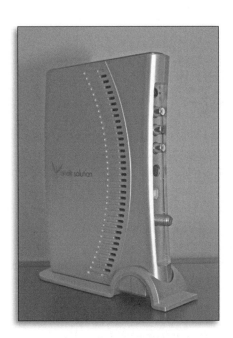

FIGURE 6.8. One device for capturing television broadcasts is the OnAir Creator, from Autumn Wave

A common feature of all these devices is that they connect to a computer via a USB connection and can receive broadcast television signals over the air or when connected to a cable or satellite television converter box with a coaxial cable. The converter box is used to receive the television signal and tune to a specific station. When the broadcast is complete, the program can be viewed on the computer and captured. In some cases, the device comes with its own software that is used either to capture still frames from the show being broadcast or to record video full-motion video clips. The software may allow you to make changes to the quality of the video and audio, as well as select where the recorded video will be saved.

DVDS

DVDs can also be a good source of educationally useful video; however, most commercial DVDs of movies or television shows contain copy-protection encryption. The process of extracting clips described here works only with DVDs not containing this anti-copying technology. Extracting a video clip from a DVD refers to rerecording a particular segment of the disc, rather than copying an entire disc. In most software designed for extracting clips from DVDs, you must set the start point, the precise place on the disc where you want the video clip to begin, and then set the end point, the precise place on the disc where you want the video clip to end. Once those parameters are selected, the software rerecords the segment, creating a new digital video file.

Commercial software that can accomplish this process includes Cinematize 2, which is commercially available for $129. Free applications that perform the same basic functions are also available, although they lack some of the more advanced features. They include MagicDisc 2.7, Ashampoo Burning Studio Free 5, AV DVD Player Morpher 3, and HandBrake 0.9 for Mac. (The AoA DVD Ripper SE 5, and the Easy DVD Ripper & Converter 3 are free to try but $35 to purchase.) The free software is probably sufficient for most educational purposes, and the free-to-try software can always be field-tested before committing to purchase.

> **USING DVDS**
>
> More information on digitizing video clips from DVDs and a sample digital video project using such clips are available online at http://site.aace.org/video/books/teaching/acquire/video4.htm.

Shooting Your Own Video with a Digital Video Camcorder

IN RECENT years, video camcorders have evolved from being very expensive devices primarily used by professional videographers to affordable, mass-market devices used by a wide array of consumers throughout the world. Camcorders that record and play back digital video are commonly found in businesses, homes, and schools and are now a feature on many cell phones. As this technology evolves, digital video recording continues to become even more affordable and easier to accomplish. In this section, the basic features of digital video camcorders are described, along with an overview of current camcorder formats recommended for use in creating educational digital video.

BASIC CAMCORDER FEATURES

Almost all digital camcorders share some common features. They all use some type of storage medium for the recorded video information. Most camcorders can also record audio along with the video, usually from either a built-in microphone or an external microphone connected to the camera. Beyond these generalities, the price of a digital camcorder is dependent on the level of sophistication of the additional features it provides. To avoid wasting money on unnecessary features, you should know which features are most important for your needs:

- *Lens.* Most consumer digital camcorders (up to $1,000) have a fixed lens permanently attached to the camera. Prices vary widely, usually correlated to the quality of the optics. More expensive camcorders have increasingly powerful and sophisticated lenses, which affects color saturation, image clarity, low-light adaptability, depth of focus control, and other attributes. Lenses can also differ in their ability to focus at a far distance (telephoto), to focus at a close distance (macro), or to change from one distance to another (zoom). Under extreme conditions, such as recording at night or from very far away, the quality of the lens might be the difference between a useful shot and a useless one. Sophisticated lenses are one of the most underutilized features of many camcorders, however. Don't pay hundreds of extra dollars for a lens that is more elaborate than you really need.

- *Viewfinder.* The viewfinder is the part of the camera you look through to see what the camcorder is recording. Many older camcorders used a through-the-lens viewfinder, which works the same as a traditional film camera. There was a transitional period during which many digital camcorders had both an electronic viewfinder and a through-the-lens viewfinder, but that is no longer the trend. More modern camcorders use only electronic viewfinders, which are actually tiny television screens that display the image the camera is seeing. More advanced viewfinders display wider ranges of motion, up to 360 degrees, so that operators can point the camera at themselves and still see the viewfinder. Be sure to try out the viewfinder on any camera you are considering for purchase and determine whether it meets your needs.

- *Focus controls.* Focus controls allow the camera to adjust the focus of the picture as it is recording. Some older cameras can only be focused manually, usually by turning a ring on the lens, whereas newer camcorders have an automatic focus feature. Consumer camcorders are usually best left with focus features set to automatic even when they do have manual overrides.

- *Exposure controls.* Exposure controls allow the camcorder to adjust the image based on the amount of light entering the lens. Most cameras have an automatic sensor that determines the proper exposure. Even though many camcorders have a manual exposure setting control, it should rarely be used. Today's increasingly sophisticated postproduction tools allow relatively easy manipulation of exposure after recording.

■ *Image capturing device.* Older video cameras used picture tubes to capture the images they were recording, but today's digital camcorders use electronic chips such as CCD (charge coupled device) and APS (active pixel sensor) that will eventually replace tube cameras entirely. The quality and size of the image capturing device is probably second only to the quality and size of the lens in influencing the price of a digital camcorder. Usually, each sensor on the image capturing device corresponds with a pixel in the resulting digital image. An image capturing device with an array of sensors 480 high by 640 wide is considered standard definition, whereas an array of sensors at least 720 high by 1280 wide is considered high definition. The maximum number of pixels contained in the captured video is directly determined by the image capturing device.

■ *AC power supply and battery.* All camcorders need power to operate. They can get their power either from an auxiliary AC power supply or from a battery. It is generally a good idea to use the AC power supply when you have access to electricity and reserve the battery for situations where no electricity is available. Some cheaper camcorders operate strictly on batteries (usually AA), but most have an input for an auxiliary AC power supply. A battery provided with a camcorder can vary in size, with a usual running time of 30 to 90 minutes. Larger batteries are often available for purchase but become increasingly heavy and expensive. A 6-hour battery might weigh almost as much as the camcorder itself and cost in excess of $200. Be sure to gauge your power needs and plan any extra costs into your budget.

> ## CAMCORDER COSTS
>
> High-definition camcorders can easily cost two to three times more than standard-definition versions offering similar features. Consider how the digital video shot on a camcorder is going to be used. If you will be playing the video on computer monitors or standard-definition television screens, a camcorder that records in high definition may not be worth the extra expense.

CREATING VIDEOS FOR ACTIVE VIEWING

By John C. Park

There is a significant difference between "home videos" and high-quality videos that can be used for active viewing and analysis, especially in the science classroom. The quality of the video should not detract from the observations, inferences, or measurements to be made by the students. The creator of the video, whether teacher or student, should use best practice to shoot the original footage for use in the classroom and for sharing with other teachers and students.

Using a tripod. Handheld video cameras usually produce shaky results. Place the digital video camera on a sturdy tripod to reduce any unnecessary camera motion. A tripod with a pan-tilt head is useful for leveling the camera and to center the event in the viewfinder. Be sure to loosen the panoramic handle of the tripod to easily pan left and right if the videotaped event might move out of the field of view of the camera. If the event will not move out of the viewfinder, be sure to center the event in the viewfinder and tighten each handle that controls panning and tilting.

Filling the screen. Videos could be viewed in a number of ways, including projection on a screen for a teacher demonstration, individual viewing on computers, or on portable handheld devices such as iPods. Adjust the optical zoom or the camera distance to fill the viewfinder with the event to be captured. Be sure that the critical parts of the event are large enough to be clearly seen on any viewing device.

Masking the background. Student attention should be directed to the event, not to the background. When possible, mask out the background using colored cardboard sheets behind the event. Also, choose a background color that will allow for the best contrast with the event. You may want to test the video on people who have color vision problems. Something that looks like a good contrast to you may not be perceived as well by others.

Timing the video. Some videotaped events last longer than the students' attention. If this is the case, create a time-lapse effect using software that will use only a fraction of the frames shot. For example, if only one out of five sequential frames will be used in the video, the event will be displayed five times faster than what the original video captured. On the other hand, if the event happens rapidly, you may want to create a slow-motion effect by adding to the sequence of frames. For example, instead of a sequence of frames 1, 2, 3, 4, the edited version may contain the sequence 1, 1, 2, 2, 3, 3, 4, 4. As a result, the movie should appear to move at one-half the original speed. These video effects can be accomplished using movie editing software, such as iMovie.

On the other hand, if you know you will want to create a time-lapse of a slow event, you may want to shoot the video at a rate other than 30 frames per second. For example, Logger Pro software allows you to shoot digital video at a frame rate of your choosing. When you shoot using a lower frame rate under fluorescent lighting, you may be surprised at the results. Some frames may appear to be lighter than others. Fluorescent lights have a flicker rate of approximately 120 cycles per second and will influence the appearance of the sequential images.

Using additional lighting. Modern digital video cameras have amazing optics that allow video to be captured with little light. However, low light levels may make the video appear grainy. Additional light will reduce this effect. When the event space is small, such as crystals precipitating in a cooling liquid contained in a test tube, you should either set up the camera very close to the event or zoom in. In either case, less light will enter the lens, and additional lighting on the event will brighten the image for better clarity. You may also need to adjust the focus if the camera is close to the event.

(continued)

Adjusting sound clarity. For some videos, both sound and motion are important. When sound is included in the video, think about how to improve its quality. Shooting a video with high-quality sound is easier than editing sound problems out of the movie. Most digital video cameras have built-in microphones that work well when the event is near the camera. External wireless microphones would be useful for events that are farther away from the camera. Be aware of other noises, such as air vents, overhead fans, and animal noises, that could be a distraction in the video or that could degrade the quality of what is to be heard.

Sharing your product. If you plan to share your video with other teachers, you may want to produce a few different versions so they can use it differently. Some teachers may not wish to use the questions you included in the movie title pages and would like to edit the movie using their own questions. Or perhaps others would not want to use the audio you use in your class and would prefer to create their own audio track. Still others may want to use a portion of your video in an online test. Create transportable video that others could repurpose into new activities.

TYPES OF DIGITAL CAMCORDER RECORDING FORMATS

Digital camcorders come in many different types and price ranges, depending greatly on the sophistication of the features previously described. An additional feature that deserves discussion is the recording format used by the camcorder.

FIGURE 6.9. A mini-DV tape.

Mini-DV camcorders. A large number of camcorders record video onto a tape cassette, one much smaller than a VHS tape. Many digital camcorders record video onto mini-DV (digital video) tapes (Figure 6.9), which generally allow recording of either 60 or 120 minutes, depending on which of the two quality settings is used. The mini-DV format is still a popular choice for those just starting out with digital video or those who have inherited an older camcorder. Mini-DV camcorders have become one of the cheapest entry points into standard-definition recording and can be found under $200. One disadvantage of mini-DV is that the video must be transferred to the computer's hard drive, which can be a time-consuming process. However, an advantage of this format is that the tapes can be easily stored, which can be useful when important video material needs to be preserved.

Flash memory card camcorders. Flash memory camcorders record to a flash memory card, a common storage medium for digital information that includes a variety of different types from different manufacturers, including secure digital (SD) cards, memory sticks, and compact flash (CF) cards. These media make the video recordings easily portable, as the memory cards can be replaced to increase recording capability and can also be moved to other devices, such as computers equipped with memory card readers. An advantage of flash memory card camcorders is that the footage can be transferred to a computer's hard drive from the flash memory card as a folder full of data files. This is a much faster transfer process than capturing footage, as is required with mini-DV tapes. Further, specific video clips can be transferred individually for maximum efficiency.

Hard disk drive camcorders. Hard disk drive (HDD) camcorders, as the name implies, record video information onto a hard disk built into the camcorder. As with a computer, the information is stored internally, and no external medium is required for the video recording. Many HDD camcorders also include the ability to record to a memory card, so you have two choices for storing the video you shoot. This type of dual recording format is generally marketed as a hybrid camcorder. Like flash memory card camcorders, hard disk drive camcorders can be treated just like an external hard drive by your computer. The process of transferring files to your local hard drive from the camcorder then becomes almost identical to the process of transferring video clips from a USB thumb drive. Similar to the flash memory camcorder, you can transfer entire folders of video clips, or select individual clips to copy.

Mini-DVD camcorders. Some digital video camcorders can record directly to a mini-DVD. The major advantage of recording video on mini-DVDs is that the finalized disc can be played back on most standard DVD players, as well as on computers with a DVD drive. Recordings can then easily be stored on these small discs for later use or for more permanent archiving. However, once a disc has been finalized, it cannot be reused. Some digital camcorders are available that can record to both a mini-DVD and a memory card. DVD camcorders had a period of popularity, but they have now generally been replaced in the market by camcorders that record directly to a flash drive, hard disk drive, or hybrid combination.

Ultraportable camcorders. Like many other technological devices, digital video camcorders have become smaller and less expensive. Ultraportable camcorders, such as the wildly popular Flip Video cameras, are scaled down in terms of features, because they record video of moderate quality to an internal memory chip. However, connecting the camcorder to a computer to transfer the video is simple via the camera's built-in USB connector. The combination of low price, ease of use, and portability has helped make these devices currently among the best-selling camcorders available. If you are unsure that the moderate image quality of the Flip Video will suit your needs, perusing the many YouTube videos demonstrating the use of the Flip should provide guidance.

Digital still cameras. Many digital still cameras include the capability of shooting video, potentially eliminating the need to own both a digital camera and a digital camcorder. Although the quality of the video shot with one of these cameras may not be as good as with a dedicated digital camcorder, the convenience and reduced cost of having a single piece of equipment may be attractive for many teachers and students. In addition, some digital cameras that record video also include software for easily uploading videos to YouTube.

Conclusion

AS YOU can see, a wide variety of ways exist for acquiring digital video for classroom use. As with all technology, digital video technology is evolving at a dizzying pace. New software programs will continue to appear with regularity, as will new camcorder models and more powerful digital video devices. The information presented here should serve as a starting point for exploring the dynamic opportunities afforded by digital video.

Once you have acquired digital video, regardless of its source, you and your students have many exciting options for editing, remixing, and combining video to communicate the precise message you wish to convey, which is the subject of the next chapter.

> More complete information on downloading videos from YouTube and a sample digital video project using video clips may be found online at http://site.aace.org/video/books/teaching/acquire/video1.htm.

CHAPTER 7

Bernard Robin, Daniel Tillman, and Curby Alexander

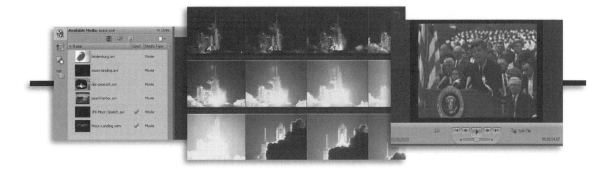

creating
digital video

USING STILL images and video clips, teachers can create their own videos to engage, inform, and challenge students, while students can create videos to explore the world around them and communicate their ideas and understandings.

Previous chapters described a number of ideas for creating video in the context of learning educational content. This chapter describes a variety of tools you can use for implementing those

projects—primarily with digital video editors. Regardless of how you acquired the video and depending on the digital video editing software you choose, you can complete the following tasks:

- Make a movie from still images alone

- Extract clips of specific scenes from longer video

- Trim or delete unwanted video footage

- Rearrange scenes in a video

- Combine multiple video clips or combine video and still images

- Add special effects and transitions to your video

- Add sounds, music, or voice-over narration to your video

- Add text-only frames or text captions to images or video

The general process for creating video is similar across video editing software programs.

1. Import your collection of images or prerecorded video into a project bin. (The software may enable you to capture video not already on your computer.)

2. Place the video(s) and/or images in the timeline or storyboard in the sequence you wish to display them.

3. If you wish, you can add special effects to video or images and transition effects between video and images. You may also add text-only slides or add text over video or images. Most programs allow you to add sound, such as music or narration, as well.

4. When you have finished creating and editing, save your video in a format that will work with a media player.

PHOTO STORY 3

Photo Story 3 is a free program available for Windows XP, Vista, and Windows 7 operating systems. Download from www.microsoft.com/windowsxp/using/digitalphotography/photostory/default.mspx.

Making Videos Using Only Still Images

A NUMBER of inexpensive and user-friendly video editing software programs are available today that make creating digital videos easier than ever before. The most basic of these programs is the wizard-based model used in applications such as Microsoft Photo Story 3, which can be used for creating a video from only still images (Figure 7.1).

To create a video from digital images with a program such as Photo Story, import the photos you want to use and arrange them in order in the timeline. Photo Story automatically adds zooming and panning motion to the pictures you import, also known as the "Ken Burns" effect (named after the filmmaker who pioneered the use of this technique in his historical documentaries). You can easily customize this motion to emphasize a particular area of the image (Figure 7.2).

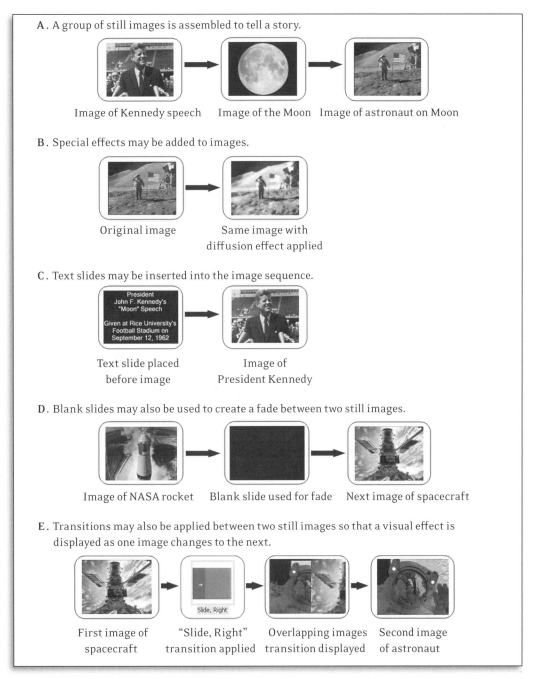

A. A group of still images is assembled to tell a story.

Image of Kennedy speech   Image of the Moon   Image of astronaut on Moon

B. Special effects may be added to images.

Original image   Same image with diffusion effect applied

C. Text slides may be inserted into the image sequence.

Text slide placed before image   Image of President Kennedy

D. Blank slides may also be used to create a fade between two still images.

Image of NASA rocket   Blank slide used for fade   Next image of spacecraft

E. Transitions may also be applied between two still images so that a visual effect is displayed as one image changes to the next.

First image of spacecraft   "Slide, Right" transition applied   Overlapping images transition displayed   Second image of astronaut

FIGURE 7.1. Making a video from still images.

The wizard-based screens in Photo Story 3 walk you through additional tasks, such as adding titles to pictures, recording audio narration with a microphone, adding music, and saving your work. When a project created in Photo Story is completed, two files are created and must be saved. The first is the project file, designated by the extension .wp3.

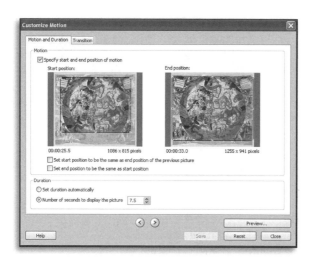

FIGURE 7.2. The Customize Motion Wizard in Photo Story 3 allows zooming and panning.

This file allows you to open the project at a later time, which may be helpful if you want to make changes to the project, add more images, correct mistakes, and so forth. The other file Photo Story saves is a video file in the Windows Media Video format (.wmv) so the completed project can be played back on a computer.

DIGITAL STORIES

One type of digital story consists of a short, personal video narrative that includes photographic and other still images as well as a musical soundtrack. If you want your students to create digital stories, the following website is a great resource: A Guide to Digital Storytelling (Center for Digital Storytelling)— www.storycenter.org/ memvoice.

Programs such as Photo Story 3 have a very specific use, which means they are not very flexible. Photo Story 3 does not allow you to include prerecorded video clips. Also, the .wp3 project file you create can be opened only in Photo Story 3. Video editing software programs, such as Windows Movie Maker or Adobe Premiere Elements, cannot open .wp3 files. The .wmv file you create with Photo Story 3 can be opened in another program, but editing in this file is difficult. You can add video to the beginning or end of the .wmv file, but editing the original video may cause disruptions with the motion, transitions, and, especially, any audio included in the Photo Story file.

Video Editing Software

MANY VIDEO projects you and your students will want to create will include full-motion video clips. A number of different software programs are available that allow you to work with video clips in what is called a "nonlinear" fashion. Nonlinear simply means that any point in a specific clip may be accessed and edited, whether it is at the beginning, the end, or any point in the middle.

TABLE 7.1. Video Editing Software Programs

PROGRAM	OPERATING SYSTEM	CHARACTERISTICS
ADOBE PREMIERE ELEMENTS	Windows	Scaled-down version of the more professional Adobe Premiere software but has most features students and educators will need
APPLE IMOVIE	Mac	Included with most new Macintosh computers or may be purchased as part of iLife suite of applications
COREL VIDEO STUDIO	Windows	Full-featured video editing program that also includes easy-to-use wizards and templates
MICROSOFT MOVIE MAKER	Windows	A component of the Microsoft Windows operating system; not as full-featured as other editing programs but has many features students and teachers will need
PINNACLE STUDIO	Windows	Scaled-down version of more professional editing software, from Avid Technology
VEGAS MOVIE STUDIO	Windows	Scaled-down version of more professional editing software, from Sony Creative Software

Some of the most popular nonlinear video editing software programs used by teachers and students are shown in Table 7.1.

COMMON FEATURES OF VIDEO EDITING PROGRAMS

Almost all digital video editing programs share some common features. They all allow users to work with one or more full-motion video clips; add still images; add titles, narration, and music; and trim video clips by deleting unwanted sections.

TIMELINE AND STORYBOARD VIEWS

Most video editing software programs provide different options for viewing and working with video clips, most commonly the timeline view (Figure 7.3) and the storyboard view (Figure 7.4). Each view provides a working layout of the media elements being used.

HOW DIGITAL VIDEO FILES ARE STRUCTURED

Full-motion video clips, like motion pictures, are actually made up of a number of still images that are displayed sequentially, one after another. Most motion pictures use 24 frames per second (FPS), which means that 24 individual still images, or frames, are used to make up one second of a movie. Like motion pictures, full-motion video clips use a sequential series of still images, although most video clips use 30 frames per second, rather than 24.

FIGURE 7.3. The bottom portion of the screen (from Adobe Premiere Elements) shows the timeline view. Note that you can see the sequence of video clips as well as the accompanying audio sequences below the video.

FIGURE 7.4. Video clips displayed in the storyboard view (called the "sceneline) in Adobe Premiere Elements. The small boxes with the diagonal stripe between clips display any transition effects that have been applied. The black square between the two clips shows that there is blank space between two video clips.

A. The clip size slider in Apple's iMovie software can be used to adjust how much or how little of a video clip is displayed in the editor.

B. A video clip in iMovie adjusted so that only a small portion is displayed.

C. The same video clip in iMovie adjusted so that a larger portion is displayed.

FIGURE 7.5A, B, C. Using the clip size slider in iMovie.

In the timeline view, you can expand or reduce the magnification of the video clips to see either more or less detail, even viewing individual frames of the video clip. You can also add video effects, audio, and text overlays in this view.

One of the most popular video editing software applications for the Macintosh is iMovie. Like Premiere Elements and Windows Movie Maker, iMovie by default displays video clips in a timeline in which one thumbnail image is shown for every five seconds of a clip. The view in iMovie may be expanded by clicking on the clip size slider (Figure 7.5A) and dragging to the right or left.

TRIMMING VIDEO

One of the main uses of video editing software is removing unwanted footage, also known as trimming the video. To trim a video clip, you need to place the video clip in the storyboard, then switch to the timeline view. Usually, you can trim the beginning of the video by dragging a vertical bar on the left to the point in the video where you would like it to begin. You trim the end of the video by dragging a bar from the right to the point where you want the clip to end. The software does not actually delete any portion of the original video clip, but instead removes portions of the clip from the timeline so that they do not show up in the final rendering of the video project. Therefore, all trimming is reversible, so long as the original file remains accessible.

When capturing footage that will later be trimmed, you may want to leave several additional seconds at both the beginning and end of the video. This way, you can include transition effects (such as cross dissolves) without losing any of the action you want viewers to see.

WORKING WITH VIDEO CLIPS

Extracting short clips from a longer video can be achieved in multiple ways. If you are not limited by hard drive space, you can capture an entire video on the computer, then trim as described in the previous section. If computer storage is limited, then capture only the sections of the video you need. This second method requires previewing the footage in order to plan in advance which portion(s) of the video to capture. To rearrange these separate scenes, use either the timeline or a storyboard view to place the clips in a sequence from left to right to determine their order of play.

ADDING SPECIAL EFFECTS

Depending on which video editing program you use, a number of special effects may be added to video or images. Effects are generally added in the storyboard view.

Most programs include a collection of preset effects that you can apply to individual clips, such as fading in and out, increasing or decreasing brightness, changing colors, aging, zooming and panning, and pixelating. You can also choose from a variety of transition effects to be placed between video clips or images. Transitions can be helpful for cluing the viewer that one clip is ending and another is beginning, which is not always necessary. If you choose to add a transition, it will begin while the first video clip is still playing and will play through the beginning of the next video.

Most programs allow you to add title and credit screens, text-only frames between clips, and text over video or images, all of which can be animated. These are usually viewed in the storyboard view.

Students can get caught up in experimenting with effects and transitions and text animations, wasting hours and sometimes even running out of time to complete their movie project. Although these effects can sometimes enhance a video, gratuitous special effects can actually distract viewers from the content. Remind your students that less is more when it comes to special effects. Special effects should be used only when necessary to augment a portion of the content or to smooth out the transition between sections of content. Students should focus first on providing interesting and useful content to communicate their message effectively.

Before beginning a video project, you might talk with students about how to prioritize their time and the relative significance of special effects and audio (discussed in the following section) to your assessment of their work. Special effects and music can seem like much more fun to students than the content they should be learning or presenting, so they will need clear direction about where to focus their time.

COPYRIGHT AND MUSIC IN YOUR VIDEOS

By Daniel Tillman

According to the Fair Use Guidelines for Multimedia (http://ccumc.org/system/files/MMFUGuides.pdf), you may use up to 10% of a song so long as it does not exceed 30 seconds and there is proper attribution. However, the Fair Use Guidelines are nonlegislative, so they in no way provide legal protection if you are sued. The only way to be completely safe is to get written permission from the copyright holder, which can be difficult and sometimes costly.

For these reasons, many video makers use music available under Creative Commons licensing. At creativecommons.org there is a section dedicated to discussing music for video (http://creativecommons.org/legalmusicforvideos), as well as a list of websites offering Creative Commons music. As an example, magnatune.com offers a wide variety of genres of music including ambient, classical, electronica, jazz, blues, metal, New Age, and rock. Their website states, "No paid license is required for people creating new works for noncommercial use." If there are any concerns, be sure to check that your project qualifies as "noncommercial use," as defined by the Creative Commons License (https://magnatune.com/info/licensing).

If you are interested in building a library of music that can become a resource for future projects, consider royalty-free music such as that offered by Digital Juice (www.digitaljuice.com). They sell digital music, under the brand name of Stack Traxx, which can be used as often as desired without additional costs after the one-time purchasing fee has been paid. Stack Traxx music is capable of masking many of the audio blemishes that are most common when recording sound with consumer video equipment.

Another alternative is to create your own songs using music loop software. Free programs such as Acid Xpress (www.acidplanet.com/downloads/xpress) allow users to generate songs quickly out of specialized music clips that can be seamlessly looped together. Acid Xpress, and programs like it, can automatically match the pitch and tempo of the music clips selected for a song, thereby helping to ensure that even nonmusicians can generate satisfactory soundtracks for their videos. In addition, a wide variety of compositions that have been produced by the community of music loop software users are often available through the same websites that distribute the loops.

For more on copyright and fair use, see Appendix B.

ADDING AUDIO

Most video editing programs allow you to add music, sounds, and voice-over narration. You must import audio files into the program's project bin and then add and view them from the timeline view. Within these programs, you can usually at a minimum adjust the volume, mute, fade in, and fade out.

Audio is best used to channel the attention of the audience toward the portions of the content that deserve highlighting. Similar to special effects, music and sounds can either focus attention on the key components of the movie or distract the viewer from the point of the message.

Remind students to keep the volume of background music low enough that it does not overwhelm dialogue or narration in the video. You might also note that narration can provide useful information to the viewer, but if it merely describes what is clearly visible in the video image, it is rarely an improvement.

SAVING AND EXPORTING EDITED VIDEO

Most video editing programs save your work as a project file with a filename extension proprietary to the program you are working in. In Photo Story 3, all of the components— images, text, narration, music, transitions, and effects—are included in the project file you save (.wp3 file). The project files for nonlinear video editors contain only the *instructions* for how the various components will work together, but do not contain any of the images, audio, or video clips. This is an important difference in the way these two kinds of software programs work. You must make sure that all of the media used in the video editing project are saved in the proper location in order for the project to open properly for additional editing. In practice, this means that when you use a nonlinear editor, all media assets that you have imported into the project bin are linked via a pathway that can be broken if the asset is moved or renamed. If this occurs, use the software's options to relink the assets when next opening the project file.

Another common feature of video editing programs is that they allow you to export a completed video project to other formats. Two of the most common methods of exporting edited video are saving the video for playback on a computer and creating a DVD that may be played either on a computer with a DVD drive or on a DVD player connected to a television set.

WEB-BASED VIDEO EDITORS

Several web-based applications have appeared in the past few years that let users assemble and edit videos online without the need for a separate video editing program. Although none of the current crop of online tools (see Table 7.2) approaches the level of sophistication or feature set of the stand-alone video editing programs, they are all free tools that may serve as a useful starting point for teachers interested in experimenting with digital video editing and sharing over the web.

These online resources are also important in that they provide us with a glimpse of where video editing technology may be headed in the not-too-distant future. Because they are web-based, they are able to change quickly and keep up with the new developments in video technology that are certain to come.

TABLE 7.2. Online Video Editing Sites

NAME	WEBSITE LINK
PHOTOBUCKET	http://photobucket.com
MOVIE MASHER	www.moviemasher.com
ONE TRUE MEDIA	www.onetruemedia.com

EDITING SCREENCASTS

A number of software programs are available for capturing screencasts, as described in Chapter 6: "Acquiring Digital Video," but only a couple of them available at this time include editing capability.

Camtasia Studio for Windows includes a work area with a clip bin, preview window, and timeline similar to those found in other video editing software programs (Figure 7.6). Video and audio captured with Camtasia Recorder can be edited with Camtasia Studio's editing feature.

Camtasia Studio includes many additional features that can increase the educational effectiveness of a screencast, such as captions, text labels, quizzes, and surveys that may be added to a screen recording. For example, a quiz may be created and inserted into the middle of a screencast video. The quiz will pause the video, and a question will appear on screen. Your screencast could include questions at certain points that require an answer before the screencast continues playing. As shown in Figure 7.7, you can add different types of questions including multiple choice, fill in the blank, and short answer.

Adobe Captivate for Windows is another program that can be used to create and edit high-quality screencasts. Captivate has the

SAMPLE SCREENCAST

A sample screencast created with Adobe Captivate may be found at http://site.aace.org/video/books/teaching/create/captivate/test1.htm.

FIGURE 7.6. The work area in Camtasia Studio shows the elements of the program, including the time-line at the bottom of the screen.

FIGURE 7.7. The Quiz and Survey Manager in Camtasia Studio.

added capability of working with other Adobe programs. For example, you can import images created in Adobe Photoshop.

STORYBOARDING

Some helpful web resources for classroom storyboarding can be found at

■ www.willamette.edu/wits/idc/mmcamp/Storyboard_handout.htm (Willamette University Instruction Design Center website)

■ www.storycenter.org/memvoice/pages/cookbook.html (Center for Digital Storytelling website)

Tips for Student-Created Video Projects

WHEN CREATING video, students will likely benefit from some scaffolding to ensure that they work efficiently, stay on task, and successfully complete their assignment.

For most types of video, a storyboard is an absolute necessity. A storyboard is simply a hand-drawn or digital sequence of images to help with planning and visualizing a video. Some teachers feel this step is so important that they make students "sell" the storyboard to them before filming and editing.

Occasionally, video created by students will bear the marks of natural creativity and cleverness, but making good movies is hard. Knowing that even the professionals make their share of flops, you should have realistic expectations about the quality of filming, editing, storytelling, and depth of understanding that will be portrayed in student-created videos. Some teachers have found that student videos more often resemble encyclopedia entries than creative and insightful treatments of a topic. Showing exemplary videos may help students better envision the qualities that will be most important in the videos they make.

In addition, though students are often engaged by creating video, they can easily become focused on style rather than substance and lose sight of the primary goal of the assignment. They may become seduced by the variety of options for background music, transitions, and special effects or become obsessed with cropping images just so. The following tips can help you better support student video production and improve the chances that your instructional objectives will be met:

- Students will need to have familiarity with video editing or moviemaking software, as well as an understanding of the fundamental steps involved in the video editing process. These steps include moving files from the video camera to a computer, as well as any other content—including music and still images—that will become part of the final video. Students will also need to have basic computer skills, such as the ability to properly save files and keep track of file locations. As a way to anticipate these technical issues, you should complete a video project of your own from beginning to end on a computer students will be using. If this is your first video project, the final movie can also serve as an example for students to view.

- Students need basic understanding of the language of video editing (e.g., pan, zoom, timeline view, storyboard view, and roughcut). Becoming familiar with the vocabulary of video editing can enhance a group's ability to collaborate on their projects. Consider creating a handout or poster with visuals and the corresponding terminology to which students can refer as needed.

- Assign roles to all the members of the video-making team, such as storyboard creator, camera operator, video editor, and soundtrack musician. Typical cooperative group strategies should be applied for maintaining the most productive workflow.

- Take advantage of peer expertise. Most likely, you will have a few students who already possess experience with video and other digital media. These students can help students who are less experienced.

- Formative assessment at every stage is key to a successful final project. Beginning video makers often make the mistake of thinking that they should not show their work-in-progress, but instead show only the final product. The weakness of this approach is that it greatly diminishes the capacity to fix problems before the video is finalized. Teacher review of and feedback about the videos while they are still in the development stage can help ensure quality control.

AGE-SPECIFIC STRATEGIES

GRADES K-3

- Young students will be excited about having participated in the moviemaking process and will likely consider the end product their movie. Let students draw or capture and then narrate one or two images that will become part of a class movie. Chances are they will still meet the learning objectives for the assignment, the task will more closely resemble activities with which the students are already familiar, and the fact that they are contributing to a movie project will keep them engaged.

- Set up a "movie station," where you can work with students individually or in small groups to annotate or narrate their images. Young students are often quite diverse in terms of the technical skills they have acquired. Bringing a large group of young students to the computer lab all at one time to work on the movie will be frustrating for both you and the students. Teachers of young students will accomplish more by working in small groups while the rest of the class is engaged in a different activity. This approach will require more calendar days, but it will actually conserve class time.

GRADES 4-8

- Students in this age range are becoming more capable of mixing their own media into a unified movie project, but you may still consider putting students in small groups to work together.

- Give students clear boundaries for acquiring images or video. You may give them a set of images or video clips to choose from, or carefully choose websites with images or video they can use. Otherwise, you should provide students with a set amount of time to capture their media. Using an open-ended search engine for locating images is risky and time consuming, and it will result in projects with random and irrelevant images or video. Even adults are easily sidetracked when searching through online collections of images and video; this applies even more strongly to adolescents who may be looking for an excuse to procrastinate.

- Regarding time, less is more. One might assume that if students can capture good images in 5 minutes, then they will capture awesome images in 15 minutes, but this is rarely the case. Students will often work more efficiently if they have a limited amount of time to capture images or video. (Note: Video typically takes longer to capture than still images because of the need for multiple takes and the fact that live action is being filmed.)

- Have an activity planned for students who finish early. Consider projecting the day's objectives on the screen or printing them on a handout so that students know what to do after they have finished each step. If not told what to do next, students will create their own entertainment.

- Decide in advance which aspects of the editing process can be done in the computer lab or with a laptop cart, and which elements should be done individually or in small groups. For example, students of this age can easily import their images or video into an editing program, and many of them can apply their own postproduction effects or music. However, even with headsets, students are unlikely to create clean, high-quality narrations in a large-group setting because of the amount of room noise and distractions. Consider setting up a recording station in a quieter spot for students to capture recordings, which can be added to the movie later.

GRADES 9–12

- High school students are capable of creating movies independently or in small groups. Although younger students are likely to be naturally engaged by video projects, high school students may no longer be interested in making movies. Do not assume that giving these students cameras or a list of web-based digital image collections will naturally excite them to make a movie. Carefully consider how you will present the project, the amount of student freedom in the projects, and the learning objectives.

- Whereas students in Grades 4–8 may need time constraints in terms of making the video, high school students will need strict limits on the duration of the final product. Challenge students to make tough editing decisions in order to stay within the time limit.

- Clearly establish which content objectives are to be demonstrated through the movies, and provide examples for students to view. If the learning objectives are not clear, students will create movies intended solely to entertain each other. Exemplary movies can and should be entertaining, but the learning objectives must also be demonstrated with proficiency.

- Allow students freedom in acquiring images. Students at this age should be able to use search engines or capture their entire project with a still or video camera. They are also more likely to put more time into the project than you can allot during school hours. You may consider providing extra lab hours before or after school or during lunch to accommodate students who want to work more on their videos.

- Establish clear expectations regarding the use of copyrighted material. Students this age know how to—and likely will—use copyright-protected materials in their projects unless instructed otherwise. These materials include music, images, and video clips. Teachers should require students to provide a reference for every media source used, and they may want to consider having students use only media they create themselves or obtain through a Creative Commons license.

> ### SKYPE
>
> If an invited guest expert cannot attend in person, try a conference call or an online videoconference using a program such as Skype.

VIDEO PROJECT ASSESSMENT

Assessment should, of course, be aligned with learning outcomes. Unless you are teaching a filmmaking course, your evaluation should place only limited emphasis on the aesthetic qualities of the video, especially for students at younger ages. Because students may lack the technical skill to make a movie that fully communicates all they understand about the targeted concepts, they should be able to demonstrate the target learning outcome both through the movie itself and through associated discussion or a learning journal completed throughout the project. Final class presentations should not only show and tell but should include facilitated discussions to further probe student understanding. You might even invite an expert on the topic to facilitate discussion initiated by the student films.

Security Issues and Student-Created Digital Video

STUDENTS ESPECIALLY enjoy video projects when they provide choice, creativity, ownership, and opportunities to communicate with a peer audience. Depending on your goals and school policy, that peer audience may extend beyond a single classroom to others within the school, to family and friends, or to the general public.

When students create digital videos, you may have the opportunity to share them with a broader audience through a website or blog. If you choose to publish your students' work on the web, you will need to consider some security issues:

- Foremost, you will need to research your school district's policies regarding acceptable use of technology. This policy will vary among states and school districts. Some school districts allow student work to be published on the web with parent permission, whereas others strictly prohibit it.

- If your school district allows student work to be published on the web, make sure you obtain parent permission for each student. Clearly explain the nature of the project and why you want to share student work with a wider audience.

Many school districts have parents sign a form at the beginning of the school year granting permission for general technology use. Look closely at this document to see if it includes a section on publishing student work on the web. If not, you will need to obtain parental permission specific to your project. Even if the general form gives permission for putting student work on the web, you should inform parents at the onset of the project of what you are doing and how the work will be shared. Some parents may have signed the form without carefully reading each section.

- If students are not permitted to be included in movies published on the web, they can still participate in the project by fulfilling roles behind the camera. You should exclude their names from all credits and other text accompanying the movie. Even if you do not agree with the parents' rationale for not allowing their child to participate, you must honor their wishes and remove all identifying information about that student from the movie.

- Students, especially when they are in a performance context, will be tempted to amuse each other. The video projects should be fun, but you also want them to reflect student learning. The wider a movie's audience, the larger the pool of people that might be offended by misguided attempts at humor. Encourage students to avoid reinforcing stereotypes, singling out individuals or groups of people for humorous reasons, or mimicking inappropriate movies, shows, or people from pop culture. If you establish clear product standards at the beginning of the project, students will be more likely to stay close to the project's learning objectives.

- Make sure students are legally using all media in their movies. They likely know how to obtain copyrighted music, images, and video clips, but just because they know how to find something does not mean those objects are appropriate for a school-sanctioned project. If necessary, provide media or links to websites with Creative Commons-licensed media for them to use. As a way to completely avoid copyright infringement, require all media in the movies to be completely original. This will also give students with artistic or musical abilities the opportunity to showcase their talents.

- You can post student movies on public websites such as YouTube if you have parental permission to do so, but for viewing them in class, you may want to embed the movies in a class web page, rather than watching directly from the YouTube site (for reasons outlined in Chapter 6: "Acquiring Digital Video"). The algorithms used by hosts such as YouTube are complex, but they do not actually know the content of your student's movies. The host may erroneously suggest movies that are totally unrelated to your students' movies, causing unnecessary distraction or suggesting something entirely inappropriate.

If you embed the video from YouTube, first uncheck the box on the YouTube screen that allows other videos to be suggested after the video is through playing (see Chapter 6 for a full explanation of embedding YouTube videos safely).

By following these suggestions, you will communicate to your students, parents, administrators, and the broader audience that these movies were made with integrity and that the students' learning was the primary aim of the project.

Conclusion

MANY MODERN video editors provide the option to use easy-to-follow wizard-based programs and increasingly simple user interfaces. As a result, working with digital video is more manageable than ever before. As technical obstacles to creating digital videos continue to decrease, you and your students can focus more energy on achieving higher standards of content quality. As long as the message and purpose of the content drive all creative decisions, making digital videos can bring real-life relevance and greater engagement to learning projects across the curriculum.

CHAPTER 8

*Glen L. Bull, Daniel Tillman,
and Lynn Bell*

communicating
with digital video

THROUGHOUT THIS book you have seen a wide array of ways to communicate with digital video in educationally effective ways. The videos our authors have recommended include everything from home movies on YouTube, to segments from Hollywood dramas and professionally produced documentaries, to student-created works.

To keep the lines of communication open with your students, the best educational video is often brief, interesting, and mentally stimulating (which may eliminate a large portion of the recorded lectures often available on educational video sites). It should promote student engagement, or analysis, or knowledge acquisition/retention, or skill acquisition, or conceptual understanding, or critical thinking.

Obviously, picture and sound quality needs to be clear; the subject must be large enough to see well, with few extraneous visual distractions; and the components of the action need to be accessible in order for viewers to make reliable interpretations (especially for viewers with limited prior knowledge).

Most importantly, the videos you show in your classroom should be connected to the curriculum. Table 8.1 presents some characteristics of useful educational video by content area. These criteria may be helpful as you decide among a range of possible video options for your classroom.

TABLE 8.1. Some Characteristics of Educational Digital Video by Content Area

SOCIAL STUDIES	MATHEMATICS	SCIENCE	ENGLISH/ LANGUAGE ARTS
• Portrays a significant real-time or reenacted event in history or politics • Provides visual and factual information about places, cultures, and human behavior • Presents historical information with or without interpretation • Illustrates targeted cultural characteristics through story • Serves as primary source for an authentic inquiry • Describes spatial relationships • Conveys political or civic ideas and beliefs	• Presents a context for mathematical conjecture, inquiry, and problem solving • Provides a medium for measurement and analysis • Captures connections among mathematical relationships • Exemplifies real-world applications of mathematics • Provides a creative means for mathematical communication	• Presents a context for scientific inquiry • Captures visual (and audio) data for further observation and analysis • Portrays natural phenomena that may otherwise be too fast, too slow, too small, or too far away for students to see • Provides targeted factual information in an engaging manner	• Presents enactments of written texts to enhance comprehension and facilitate practice of literary interpretation • Exemplifies a new form of communication for composition or analysis • Provides context for student inquiry and critical thinking • Provides a dynamic bridge into literary themes, global connections, visual literacy, and multimodal composition

Effective Teaching with Digital Video

MOST TEACHERS have turned on an instructional videotape or DVD in their classroom and stepped aside until the movie ended. (Many have also observed a student or two losing consciousness during this period.) The authors of this book have suggested a different way of teaching with digital video: showing one or more targeted snippets of videos so that you stay involved in the instructional process and keep students more engaged as well.

With increasing ease of use and accessibility of digital video, many teachers are discovering through serendipity and trial-and-error the most effective instructional techniques for using it in their classrooms. Although the definitive research on best practices for communicating with digital video has not yet been conducted, over the years educators have been exploring effective uses of moving images in the classroom, some dating back to the days of filmstrips. Their findings are often transferable to digital video, as these examples illustrate:

- "Film" used in combination with other instructional materials is better than either alone (Hoban & van Ormer, 1951). In other words, video should *supplement* your good instruction, not replace it.

- The most effective videos will be closely matched to your instructional goal. Video can entertain students and fill class time. Video that will enhance learning must be purposefully selected to inform, reinforce, motivate, or engage (Dale, 1969). We would add that shorter video clips (5 minutes or less) may often best fulfill this principle.

> **TEACHING TIP**
>
> Over time you may accumulate video clips in the same way that you develop a portfolio of other teaching resources. Large-capacity USB drives make it easy to transport folders of video clips from classroom to classroom in a way that would have been impractical in previous eras.

- Videos are more effective when students receive prior instruction about what to look for or what questions will be raised or answered in the video (Dale, 1969). Debriefing students after viewing will allow you to determine whether they learned what you wanted them to learn or noticed what you wanted them to notice.

The field of cognitive science offers more recent implications for using digital video to communicate effectively in the classroom. Jeffrey Zacks, a scientist at Washington University, and his research team have investigated the ways in which moving pictures are processed by the neural system. The act of watching a moving image entails significantly more complexity than viewing one or more still images. Their research indicates that under some circumstances, viewing video and animation can actually result in *decreased* comprehension in comparison with viewing equivalent still images. This decreased comprehension may occur because the viewer must interpret an ongoing stream of information. The complexity of this task can overwhelm novice viewers, who have trouble deciding which attributes to focus on.

As viewers watch an ongoing stream of visual information, it appears that their brains segment the information into meaningful events and encode it in memory that way. This information suggests that you may be able to facilitate knowledge retention and understanding by highlighting key events in the video.

Another researcher, Barbara Tyversky, notes that when viewers do not know where to focus attention, they find the information difficult to process and, consequently, difficult to remember. She suggests that interactivity can be an important strategy for improving comprehension. You can start and stop video at key points, replaying segments that need review while skipping parts that students already understand.

Digital video lends itself to these instructional strategies, allowing you to create bookmarks in the media player that correspond to key events and conceptual boundaries. During whole-class instruction, you can serve as a mediator, highlighting key events, checking student understanding, or soliciting predictions about what will happen next. When students are viewing video individually or in small groups, you can insert strategic pause points to provide opportunities for students to process and assimilate the video.

Communicating via Social Media

PERSPECTIVES ON classroom uses of video in the past were shaped by tools such as the filmstrip projector and videotape player. But digital video and new Web 2.0 social media tools allow communication involving digital video to take place in less traditional ways than those discussed previously in this chapter.

In classroom settings, there are a variety of ways teachers and students can share, view, and discuss video content online either individually or in small groups. These may include a class web page, a blog ("web log"), a wiki, or a social bookmarking site. Because these tools require Internet access, they are appropriate for cases in which students have access to the web. In some cases this access may be provided through a computer lab or a laptop cart. In other cases, students may have access to the Internet outside the classroom through sites such as the public library.

CLASS WEB PAGE

A traditional (or Web 1.0) web page—one that must be created offline using authoring software such as Adobe Dreamweaver—is an appropriate medium for one-way transmission of information. You may use this type of web page for accumulating related videos on a specific topic.

Depending on the sources of the videos and your technical expertise, you may do any of the following:

- Embed a video player on the web page for playing your own or students' videos

- Provide a link to your videos that will be played outside your web page on a player such as QuickTime or Windows Media Player

- Embed videos from another website, such as TeacherTube or YouTube, on your web page (to learn how, see Chapter 6: "Acquiring Digital Video")

- Provide links to go to another website to view videos

You can organize these video resources on your web page hierarchically or chronologically and provide explanatory text with each. Viewing all the videos from a single web page has the advantage of limiting distractions associated with going to a variety of other sites for viewing.

A class web page about simple machines, for example, might discuss each of the machines in an appropriate hierarchical order (Figure 8.1).

FIGURE 8.1. Frame from a video about simple machines embedded with its player (note the player controls at the bottom).

Because a screw is a specialized instance of an inclined plane, the video introduction to the inclined plane might be placed first on the page, along with accompanying text explanation. Perhaps something like this:

Simple machines can be easier to remember if you group similar ones. For example, a screw is an instance of an inclined plane that is wrapped around a cylinder.

BLOG

A blog (an abbreviation of "web log") is a Web 2.0 tool. You can create and edit the page completely online using your web browser. As the word *log* might imply, a blog consists of a series of reverse chronological entries related to specific threads or topics identified by the moderator. Usually, a blog is moderated by one individual (or sometimes a small group), and readers may respond via comments to the moderator and to each other. Entries may consist of text, images, and video. The most recent entry in a thread shows up first, followed by previous entries. Popular and easy-to-use blog sites on the web include WordPress, Blogger, and Edublogs.

A blogging platform such as WordPress allows you to construct web pages without extensive technology expertise. However, the primary advantage of blogs is the ease with which users can write or read a series of journal-type entries about one or more videos, thus participating in online discussion.

WIKI

A wiki is also a Web 2.0 tool and consists of documents or web pages that can be created collaboratively within a group of any size, designated by the creator. Wikipedia is the most famous wiki, but you can create your own and limit the group of people who have access to it. In a blog, each entry in a topic (or "thread") is separate, and new entries are appended. In a wiki, on the other hand, there is one page per topic that can be continuously revised or expanded by multiple creators/editors. Wikis may be useful tools for students working collaboratively on group projects. Sites for creating wikis include Google Sites (sites.google.com), where users can create and post collaborative web pages (Figure 8.2).

For example, a wiki created for a science class that is exploring simple machines would allow pairs or small groups of students to each create a page for a different machine (pulley, lever, wheel and axle, etc.), with an explanation consisting of video and explanatory text. Wikis include tracking features with which a teacher could easily follow the contributions of each class member.

FIGURE 8.2. Screenshot from Google Sites, an example of a wiki website.

SOCIAL BOOKMARKING

Social bookmarking sites such as Digg (www.digg.com) and Delicious (formerly del.icio. us; now www.delicious.com) provide a way for teachers and students to share and jointly annotate existing web resources they have found useful. Diigo (www.diigo.com), another bookmarking site, offers educator accounts for K–12 teachers to set up groups. A forum within the social bookmaking site lets class members not only view a particular shared video, but also discuss it within the group.

Social bookmarking sites can involve less overhead than blogs or wikis. For example, using our simple machine context, rather than ask students to create separate complete pages with video and accompanying explanatory text for each simple machine on a wiki, you can simply ask them to identify and bookmark video showing real-life examples of simple machines.

These sites provide a way to identify and catalog shared resources, which could serve as a precursor to a class web page or wiki. Annotation features on sites such as Diigo allow you and your students to comment on which video examples appear to offer the best illustrations.

OTHER OPTIONS FOR SHARING AND DISCUSSING VIDEO

The examples of blogs, wikis, and social bookmarking sites discussed here are only a fraction of the social networking tools currently emerging. For example, the initial "Bookmark and Share" option on the TeacherTube site lists more than a dozen options on an initial screen—and 50-plus more options on subsequent screens (see Figure 8.3).

FIGURE 8.3. List provided by TeacherTube of some social networking venues for sharing the site's videos.

The variety of options can seem overwhelming, but in practice, a class is unlikely to make use of more than two or three of these, such as shared bookmarks and discussion groups. The specific social media mechanisms will depend on their educational appropriateness.

VIDEOS STUDENTS MIGHT CREATE FOR VARIOUS INSTRUCTIONAL PURPOSES

By Lynn Bell

The variety of ways students might communicate through videos they create is ever increasing. The following table gives just of a few of the possibilities.

INSTRUCTIONAL PURPOSE	EXAMPLES
Demonstrate knowledge/understanding or skill acquisition; demonstrate synthesis and application of knowledge/understanding	• Documentary or informational • News-style reports • Animations or stop-motion • How-to videos or simulated teaching • Advertisements, infomercials, or book trailers • Screencasts • Music videos
Serve as a creative work	• Digital stories • Screenplays
Set up a context for a problem to be solved/ challenged/inquired about	• Story problems • Unsolved mysteries
Collect visual/audio data for observations, or analysis or to document events	• Interviews • Landmarks or geographic features • Natural objects or events • Music, dance, drama, or readings • Athletic skills • Vocational skills

For classroom or personal viewing, students' digital videos may be stored on a computer hard drive, a portable drive, a DVD or CD, a handheld device such as an iPod Touch, or a cell phone. However, you may want to create opportunities for student electronic discussion around the videos, or you may want to share them with broader audiences. If this is the case (and depending on school policy) you may want to upload videos to a class web page or to a video repository such as YouTube or TeacherTube, or to a blog or wiki where students can post comments.

SYNCHRONOUS SHARING

All of the social networking examples discussed so far involve *asynchronous* sharing, where participants create posts at different times. In this format, class participation can be extended so that a student in a study hall or library period can log on and contribute. It also allows a discussion to evolve over time in order that students can build on the foundation of earlier comments.

Another option involves *synchronous* sharing, in which students comment while they watch the video. This form of simultaneous conversation is sometimes referred to as "back-channel" discussion. Laptop carts or classroom sets of handheld devices such as the iPod Touch make this strategy feasible in some circumstances.

A back channel is an online, synchronous dialogue that appears alongside spoken words, digital video, or presentations. Back channels typically provide participants with a public and open venue for discussing presented content in a manner that minimizes disturbances and maximizes collaborative participation.

Some web-based videoconferencing and live video streaming applications, such as Elluminate (www.elluminate.com) and Ustream (www.ustream.tv), incorporate their own back-channel tools. You can also find stand-alone tools that facilitate back-channel discussion, such as CoverItLive (http://coveritlive.com) and Meebo (www.meebo.com).

Incorporating a back channel into a video viewing experience potentially serves a number of educational objectives:

- *Engagement.* Watching video is a relatively passive but complex experience that requires an audience to assimilate a range of inputs. Using back-channel discussion while viewing video creates a forum for posing questions, delivering clarifications, and engaging with the visual/auditory stimulus.

- *Increased accessibility for all learners.* Individuals who fear public speaking in face-to-face situations can thoughtfully compose and deliver insights that would not ordinarily be shared.

- *Formative assessment.* When back-channel commentary can be saved, it offers the opportunity to review questions and issues raised by the students during the presentation.

- *Global participation.* Online back channels allow people from geographically distant areas to engage in the conversation surrounding digital video.

Although there are potential advantages to back-channel communication, there are also significant educational issues that need to be considered. Providing students with back-channel tools to support synchronous dialogue while a video is playing may also distract and divide their attention. Research on conditions under which such use might be effective has not yet been conducted.

Conclusion: The Future of Digital Video

IN 1878, Eadweard Muybridge, the father of the motion picture, took a series of pictures of a galloping horse to determine whether all four hooves left the ground at the same time. Muybridge later projected the series of images, mounted on a series of glass frames, through a lens to create the first motion pictures. Remarkably, these first moving images from the 19th century are now available through the California Museum of Photography website (www.cmp.ucr.edu).

These initial moving pictures captured by Muybridge (Figure 8.4) involved months of development and research. A gathering of any size today includes several individuals who have cell phones with video capabilities. Digital video has become ubiquitous, woven into the social fabric as a casual means of ongoing communication. Emerging technologies are transforming digital movies into countless forms far beyond any that Muybridge might have imagined.

Today, both teachers and students can easily acquire video with a smartphone, edit the video on the phone, and communicate with others by sharing the edited video either offline or online via traditional web pages or a variety of social networking sites. By combining their technical, pedagogical, and content knowledge, teachers today have opportunities for teaching with video that would have seemed like science fiction in the era of the filmstrip.

Source: http://commons.wikimedia.org/wiki/File:Muybridge_race_horse_gallop.jpg

FIGURE 8.4. A photo sequence by Eadweard Muybridge of a race horse galloping. First published in 1887 at Philadelphia. (Human and Animal Locomotion, plate 626, Thoroughbred bay mare "Annie G." galloping.)

Instructional strategies for integrating digital video will continue to emerge as the technological capabilities evolve. *Teaching with Digital Video* merely serves as a starting point for innovative teachers and technology coordinators thinking about how students can learn by watching, analyzing, and creating digital video across the curriculum.

References

Dale, E. (1969). *Audiovisual methods in teaching.* New York, NY: Dryden Press.

Hoban, C. F., & van Ormer, E. B. (1951) *Instructional Film Research 1918–1950* (Technical Report No. SDC 269-7-19). University Park, PA: Pennsylvania State College.

APPENDIX A

glossary

applet. A small software program (or application) that can run in a web browser.

back channel. An electronically mediated conversation that takes place at the same time as a live or video-recorded presentation.

bandwidth. The amount of electronic data that can be transferred from one point to another, usually expressed as bits (of data) per second. A high bandwidth is required for transmitting large files, such as digital video.

bin. In some video editing software the "bin" refers to the folder in which media for a specific video project are collected before being placed in the video storyboard. The bin does not contain the actual media itself, but, rather, stores information about the location of the media. Thus, if you delete content from the bin, you are not deleting the actual media file, just the link to that media file.

blog. An abbreviation for "web log," a blog is a website that allows users to add ongoing text entries from one or more authors. All entries are saved and appear in reverse chronological order. Images and videos can also be added to most blog sites. (See Chapter 8 for an expanded definition.)

critical viewing/critical media literacy. The ability to apply critical analysis to media. Critical viewing may include interpreting the message, identifying stylistic mechanisms used by the creator, examining social influences on the message, and comparing and contrasting the media presentation with reality. (See Introduction for an expanded discussion.)

digital story. A short, personal video narrative that includes photographic and other still images and a musical soundtrack.

digital video. Video that is converted into a long series of 0s and 1s when it is recorded. This enables digital video files to be copied repeatedly without any degradation in quality, because each copy is a clone of the original. This can be contrasted with analog video, where each successive copy introduces a level of degradation to the image and sound quality.

flexible format. The ability to format a digital video to multiple video streams simultaneously regardless of the original image types (standards), formats (e.g., resolutions), and frame rates.

Geometer's Sketchpad. A dynamic construction, demonstration, and exploration software program developed by Key Curriculum Press with which users can build and investigate mathematical models, objects, figures, diagrams, and graphs.

live streaming. A live broadcast that is streamed to viewers (see *streaming video*).

multimodal writing. Writing that incorporates two or more modes of communication, such as text, images, sound, and video.

new literacies. In this book, we use new literacies primarily to refer to the ability to understand information presented across media made possible by new digital electronic technologies (including text, images, sound, video, and animation) and to communicate in these multiple modes. New literacies can also refer to the practices surrounding digital information (for example, hyperlinking) and the ethos of a more participatory, collaborative, and less author-centric manner of creating and communicating information.

mashup. Often referred to as "video mashup"; refers to a combination of video clips from multiple sources.

probeware. One or more digital measurement devices, or probes, and accompanying computer software that enables real-time digital data collection and analysis.

screencast. A digital recording of activity on a computer screen (also known as screen capture), which may include audio narration.

social networking sites. Websites that allow users to construct public or semipublic profiles about themselves, define a list (network) of others with whom they have a connection, and view information shared by others in their network. Social networking sites may include e-mail and instant message capability as well as blogs (for ongoing discussion) or wikis (for collaborative work). They may also include the capability to share images, videos, and bookmarked URLs. Popular examples include Facebook, MySpace, Twitter, WordPress, Digg, and Google Sites.

storyboard. A series of illustrations created for the purpose of planning the sequence of a motion picture.

storyboard view. A phrase used in some video editing software to describe an interface that shows thumbnails of individual video clips, as well as still images (if used) and any transitions placed between them.

streaming video. A form of delivering digital video in which the host sends the video gradually to the user's computer. Streamed video can either be prerecorded or a live broadcast. (For an expanded definition, see the section on downloading video from the web in Chapter 6.)

video clips. Short excerpts from movies, television shows, professionally prepared educational videos, or personally created videos.

video editor. A software program that enables users to edit video footage (cutting sections of video, combining multiple videos, adding text and special effects, etc.). Video editors can also facilitate translation of video from one format to another.

virtual manipulative. A digital, or computerized, version of a concrete manipulative typically used to help students learn mathematics concepts (such as blocks, rods, or bean sticks).

webcam. A digital video camera designed specifically to transmit video over the Internet.

wiki. A web-based tool that consists of documents or web pages that can be created collaboratively within a group of any size designated by the creator. (See Chapter 8 for an expanded definition.)

wizard. Refers to software programs that guide the user so that tasks may be easily completed. Most wizard-based applications use a series of dialog boxes or on-screen prompts to guide the user along a sequence of steps to perform a certain function. This type of program-based assistance can be especially useful for novice users who are unfamiliar with the software application.

YouTube. An online video repository (www.youtube.com) where digital video creators can upload and share short videos. The video collection can be searched and viewed by anyone. For a collection of short videos on how to use YouTube, see www.youtube.com/t/yt_handbook_home.

Bernard Robin

a few words about copyright
and educational fair use

Some educational projects you or your students create may contain video clips that come from movies, television shows, and news broadcasts. Technologically, locating these kinds of video clips and then reusing or remixing them to create meaningful projects has become easier every year. Video projects making use of these media resources help facilitate classroom learning and inquiry while engaging and motivating students to demonstrate their knowledge and understanding of important educational content.

Issues of ownership, copyright, permission, and educational use invariably come up in any discussion involving the use of digital video clips originally created by someone else. Chapter 6: "Acquiring Digital Video" includes a section on extracting video clips from DVDs, but as you may know, most commercial DVDs of movies contain copy protection to prevent this type of extraction. We do not advocate the breaking of copy protection on DVDs; the technique that was included in Chapter 6 was for use with the many DVDs that do not contain copy protection.

The use of copyrighted material is indeed a serious issue and one that is being studied and discussed by many educators and policy makers. Unfortunately, there is not yet a definitive answer to this question, nor is there a simple test to determine what materials you may or may not use in educational projects. You will need to try to answer the question yourself based on several factors, such as the digital medium being used; the nature of that use; the policies in place at your school or district; and, perhaps most importantly, your comfort level in using, and having your students use, material that can easily be downloaded from the web or created with commonly available hardware and software.

> **FAIR USE VIA VIDEO**
>
> To review the fundamentals of educational fair use via video, see the YouTube movie "Copyright 101 for Teachers" at www.youtube.com/watch?v=rzlry1c76nc.

All of the video clips used in projects described in the web supplement to Chapter 6 (http://site.aace.org/video/books/teaching/acquire) were designed and created by educators and students for nonprofit use. Many of the clips used in the projects are readily available on the web and were easily found and downloaded. The number of digital video clips on the web will continue to increase, and software and hardware options for working with digital video will become more available, less expensive, and easier to use.

Nonetheless, significant obstacles and challenges remain for using these kinds of digital video materials in classroom instruction. In addition to the commonly accepted practices under current copyright guidelines that allow use of copyrighted material for commentary, satire, and criticism, we hope soon to see expanded support from copyright holders and policy makers regarding the use of digital material by teachers and students. The benefits of such policies will be significant for all educators who seek to transform their students from consumers of digital video to active researchers and creators of new and exciting educational projects.

APPENDIX C

national educational technology standards

National Educational Technology Standards for Students (NETS•S)

ALL K-12 students should be prepared to meet the following standards and performance indicators.

1. **Creativity and Innovation**
   Students demonstrate creative thinking, construct knowledge, and develop innovative products and processes using technology. Students:

   a.   apply existing knowledge to generate new ideas, products, or processes

   b.   create original works as a means of personal or group expression

   c.   use models and simulations to explore complex systems and issues

   d.   identify trends and forecast possibilities

2. **Communication and Collaboration**
   Students use digital media and environments to communicate and work collaboratively, including at a distance, to support individual learning and contribute to the learning of others. Students:

   a.   interact, collaborate, and publish with peers, experts, or others employing a variety of digital environments and media

   b.   communicate information and ideas effectively to multiple audiences using a variety of media and formats

   c.   develop cultural understanding and global awareness by engaging with learners of other cultures

   d.   contribute to project teams to produce original works or solve problems

3. **Research and Information Fluency**
   Students apply digital tools to gather, evaluate, and use information. Students:

   a.   plan strategies to guide inquiry

   b.   locate, organize, analyze, evaluate, synthesize, and ethically use information from a variety of sources and media

   c.   evaluate and select information sources and digital tools based on the appropriateness to specific tasks

   d.   process data and report results

4. **Critical Thinking, Problem Solving, and Decision Making**
   Students use critical-thinking skills to plan and conduct research, manage projects, solve problems, and make informed decisions using appropriate digital tools and resources. Students:

   a. identify and define authentic problems and significant questions for investigation

   b. plan and manage activities to develop a solution or complete a project

   c. collect and analyze data to identify solutions and make informed decisions

   d. use multiple processes and diverse perspectives to explore alternative solutions

5. **Digital Citizenship**
   Students understand human, cultural, and societal issues related to technology and practice legal and ethical behavior. Students:

   a. advocate and practice the safe, legal, and responsible use of information and technology

   b. exhibit a positive attitude toward using technology that supports collaboration, learning, and productivity

   c. demonstrate personal responsibility for lifelong learning

   d. exhibit leadership for digital citizenship

6. **Technology Operations and Concepts**
   Students demonstrate a sound understanding of technology concepts, systems, and operations. Students:

   a. understand and use technology systems

   b. select and use applications effectively and productively

   c. troubleshoot systems and applications

   d. transfer current knowledge to the learning of new technologies

National Educational Technology Standards for Teachers (NETS·T)

ALL CLASSROOM teachers should be prepared to meet the following standards and performance indicators.

1. **Facilitate and Inspire Student Learning and Creativity**
   Teachers use their knowledge of subject matter, teaching and learning, and technology to facilitate experiences that advance student learning, creativity, and innovation in both face-to-face and virtual environments. Teachers:
   a. promote, support, and model creative and innovative thinking and inventiveness
   b. engage students in exploring real-world issues and solving authentic problems using digital tools and resources
   c. promote student reflection using collaborative tools to reveal and clarify students' conceptual understanding and thinking, planning, and creative processes
   d. model collaborative knowledge construction by engaging in learning with students, colleagues, and others in face-to-face and virtual environments

2. **Design and Develop Digital-Age Learning Experiences and Assessments**
   Teachers design, develop, and evaluate authentic learning experiences and assessments incorporating contemporary tools and resources to maximize content learning in context and to develop the knowledge, skills, and attitudes identified in the NETS·S. Teachers:
   a. design or adapt relevant learning experiences that incorporate digital tools and resources to promote student learning and creativity
   b. develop technology-enriched learning environments that enable all students to pursue their individual curiosities and become active participants in setting their own educational goals, managing their own learning, and assessing their own progress
   c. customize and personalize learning activities to address students' diverse learning styles, working strategies, and abilities using digital tools and resources
   d. provide students with multiple and varied formative and summative assessments aligned with content and technology standards and use resulting data to inform learning and teaching

3. **Model Digital-Age Work and Learning**
   Teachers exhibit knowledge, skills, and work processes representative of an innovative professional in a global and digital society. Teachers:
   a. demonstrate fluency in technology systems and the transfer of current knowledge to new technologies and situations
   b. collaborate with students, peers, parents, and community members using digital tools and resources to support student success and innovation
   c. communicate relevant information and ideas effectively to students, parents, and peers using a variety of digital-age media and formats
   d. model and facilitate effective use of current and emerging digital tools to locate, analyze, evaluate, and use information resources to support research and learning

4. **Promote and Model Digital Citizenship and Responsibility**

Teachers understand local and global societal issues and responsibilities in an evolving digital culture and exhibit legal and ethical behavior in their professional practices. Teachers:

   a. advocate, model, and teach safe, legal, and ethical use of digital information and technology, including respect for copyright, intellectual property, and the appropriate documentation of sources

   b. address the diverse needs of all learners by using learner-centered strategies and providing equitable access to appropriate digital tools and resources

   c. promote and model digital etiquette and responsible social interactions related to the use of technology and information

   d. develop and model cultural understanding and global awareness by engaging with colleagues and students of other cultures using digital-age communication and collaboration tools

5. **Engage in Professional Growth and Leadership**

Teachers continuously improve their professional practice, model lifelong learning, and exhibit leadership in their school and professional community by promoting and demonstrating the effective use of digital tools and resources. Teachers:

   a. participate in local and global learning communities to explore creative applications of technology to improve student learning

   b. exhibit leadership by demonstrating a vision of technology infusion, participating in shared decision making and community building, and developing the leadership and technology skills of others

   c. evaluate and reflect on current research and professional practice on a regular basis to make effective use of existing and emerging digital tools and resources in support of student learning

   d. contribute to the effectiveness, vitality, and self-renewal of the teaching profession and of their school and community

INDEX

Page references followed *t* or *f* indicate tables or figures, respectively.